Water Walkers

From Secular Careers
to Sacred Service:
39 Stories of Faith

Vince Clews

ISBN: 1530454441
ISBN-13: 978-1530454440

This book is dedicated to

My Parents
Rev. Gordon and Mrs. Eleanora Clews

ACKNOWLEDGMENTS

I would like to thank all those who have seen value in telling the stories of Christian men and women who have accepted God's call to vocational Christian service. Those thanks, of course, first go to those who contributed their stories to this book. Without their willingness to take time to fill out my questionnaire and review the drafts of their chapters, there would be no book. More to the point, when God chose them, they chose to answer, "Here am I, Lord. Send me."

I must also thank Libbye Morris. Libbye is an editor, an excellent one. And she spent more hours than should have been needed correcting my errors and refining my words. She did it because we are friends. More important, she believes that God does choose people to serve Him. I believe that God chose her for this project, and I am very grateful that she chose to serve Him.

The cover design is the result of the talent, commitment, and patience of Sandra Kenney (skenney@a1000words.com). She is also responsible for the website (www.waterwalkerstoday.com). I must have changed everything a dozen times. She is looking for a ride back across the River Styx.

The layout and design of the chapters in this book have been the work of the team at Studio 92 (www.studio92.com). Kelly and Teresa Nielsen are not only masters of their trade, they are devout Christians who cared not only about the book's appearance, but equally about its message.

I want to thank my dear friend, the Rev. Philip Burwell Roulette. Without Philip having guided me back into a relationship with the Lord, there would be no book.

And, a special thank you to my wife, Carol. Writers need people who will support them. In my case, that is literal. While I have been working on this book, Carol has continued her work as Executive Director of the Baltimore Center for Pregnancy Concerns. It is faith-based and pro-life. She works to save the lives of unborn children. And to make the lives of babies, young children, and their families better through the provision of material goods and spiritual support. I am enormously proud of her for what she does and who she is. Thank you, Lord, for this woman.

PREFACE

And straightway Jesus constrained his disciples to get into a ship, and to go before him unto the other side, while he sent the multitudes away. And when he had sent the multitudes away, he went up into a mountain apart to pray: and when the evening was come, he was there alone. But the ship was now in the midst of the sea, tossed with waves: for the wind was contrary. And in the fourth watch of the night Jesus went unto them, walking on the sea. And when the disciples saw him walking on the sea, they were troubled, saying, "It is a spirit," and they cried out for fear. But straightway Jesus spoke unto them, saying, "Be of good cheer; it is I; be not afraid." And Peter answered him and said, "Lord, if it be thou, bid me come unto thee on the water." And he said, "Come." And when Peter was come down out of the ship, he walked on the water, to go to Jesus.

Matthew 14:22–29

As the son of a Methodist minister, I was regularly exposed to this story of Peter walking on water. I heard it in multiple Sunday School classes, Sunday morning services, Sunday evening services, revivals, mission-week services, youth fellowship events, Bible studies, weddings, funerals, church camp meetings, and an assortment of other experiences.

Peter is special to *Water Walkers* for two reasons. He is at one end of a continuum you will recognize as you read the stories in this book. At the other end is Paul. Let's look first at Paul and his call to serve the Lord.

When God chose the man who would become St. Paul, he was walking the road to Damascus. Saul, as he was known then, was blinded by a great light, and a loud voice let him know in no uncertain terms that he was called.

"I am Jesus, whom you are persecuting," the Lord said. "Now get up and stand on your feet. I have appeared to you to appoint you as a servant and as a witness of what you have seen of me and what I will show you."

A blinding light and a voice as specific as that one would make "being called" remarkably easy to recognize.

At the other end of the continuum is Peter. His call came quietly as Jesus walked along the shoreline and spoke to Peter and his fellow fishermen.

"Come, follow me," Jesus said, "and I will make you fishers of men."

Modern-day Christians seldom get called to full-time vocational Christian service as directly as either Peter or Paul. True, God does speak to us, and sometimes it's very clear that He has chosen us. Yet often we find ourselves asking questions such as, "If I didn't hear it when I was an actively searching twenty-something, is it too late?" Or "Is God choosing me, or am I putting too much thought into a routine incident?" There is no one answer to questions like those.

Water Walkers is an anthology of people called after they were already into their adulthood. It is a collection of human-interest stories with a single thread: "I was chosen by God to leave what I was doing and enter full-time vocational Christian service." They are the stories of people who left careers—ones they thought would be their careers for the rest of their lives—to answer God's call. They may have had an earlier inkling that there might be some way the Lord wanted to use them, but they had moved on to secular careers. Full-time Christian service was not part of their life's plan. And then they were unmistakably "called."

This call is increasingly coming to people later in life. Seminaries are finding more and more students entering after leaving another career. In fact, today, the average age of men ordained into the Roman Catholic priesthood is in the mid-thirties.

The stories in this book demonstrate the life continuum on which God calls. Some of the stories are startling. Others deeply moving. Some without notable incident. Some even have moments of humor. All are entertaining and inspiring. In total, the stories demonstrate that God calls us in many ways, some subtle, some not so subtle. But all, at some point, clear and irrefutable.

Water Walkers does not offer a deeply spiritual analysis into the issue of callings. Nor is it a guide to biblical understanding of the matter. And it certainly is not a rallying cry for people to join the ranks of the "called." It simply shows that, on a continuum of calls, the way God delivers that message varies…and so does the way it is answered.

The stories, individually and collectively, show that God chooses people from all walks of life, each in a way that singularly touches them and makes apparent His calling.

You may find that *Water Walkers* reveals an opportunity to prayerfully consider if you are somewhere along that continuum.

Each chapter includes a scripture verse the contributor found particularly meaningful and wishes to share with readers. Perhaps you will find that you share a love of the same special verse.

As I finalized this book, I was struggling with a title for the collection of stories that follows. I have a habit of putting sticky notes on the wall in front of my desk. The wall is a mess. The most recent notes are title ideas for this particular volume. As I stuck each one to the wall, I thought, "That's a keeper. Yeah, I like that one." Then, as I pushed closer to finalizing the book, I pulled slips of paper off the wall and placed them in a folder labeled "Not this one." Nothing seemed to capture, in a phrase, what I wanted to say about the people featured in this volume and what connected them with one another.

Then, as I was working on the stories, my brother, Carter, gave me a book by Mark Batterson titled *The Grave Robber*. I was particularly struck by Batterson's remarks about Matthew 14:22–29, when Peter walked on water. Yes, Peter took only a few steps before he began to sink. But Peter did get out of the boat. He was willing to act on faith. And, for his faith, Peter walked on water.

Water Walkers is about Christian men and women who, in faith, left the safety of the boat, stepped out onto the water, and walked on it. For the people in these stories, "stepping out of the boat" meant leaving the lives they thought they were destined to live and careers they assumed were lifelong. Because God had other plans.

Here are the stories of these water walkers.

TABLE OF CONTENTS

> *"Every calling of God is personally tailor-made to the*
> *individual, and God knows exactly the right fit for*
> *each person. He even takes into account what you*
> *like doing. It's a matter of discerning the calling."*
> —*Dedi Whitaker*
> *Friend and Servant of God*

FOREWORD

I love testimonies. Testimonies build us up. They encourage us. They show us how God can work through the likes of you and me. They show us how God can use even the brokenness, failure, and pain of our lives and how by His grace he can move us to new trust, obedience, and fruitfulness. Testimonies are a gift from God.

In *Water Walkers*, Vince Clews recounts the experiences of dozens of devoted followers of Jesus who would, I suspect, consider themselves to be pretty ordinary folks. Yet by their surrender to the Lord's call, He has used them in glorious ways for His Kingdom.

So prepare to be encouraged as you read this book. And invite the Lord to challenge you through these stories to step out of the boat into the fullness of His calling on your life, as well.

The Rt. Rev. John Guernsey
Bishop, Diocese of the Mid-Atlantic
Anglican Church in North America

1

DAVID DAVIS
Broadway to God's Way
Founder, Kehilat Hacarmel

*For He Himself is our peace, who has made the two
one and has destroyed the barrier, the dividing wall of
hostility, by abolishing in His flesh the law with its
commandments and regulations. His purpose was to
create in himself one new man out of the two, thus
making peace.*

Ephesians 2:14–15

"One night after a performance on Broadway, I went
home, and a thought came to me: 'My life doesn't mean
anything!' I knew I was lost and my life truly didn't mean a
thing."

This startling revelation seemed almost impossible for
a man who had accomplished what David Davis had in a
lifetime of successes. He was a good enough athlete to play
football for the Far East Navy–Marine All-Star Team and
later at Wake Forest University. When an injury took
athletics away from David, he turned to acting and, once
again, succeeded beyond what he could have imagined. His
life was a showcase of not just reaching his goals, but
prevailing. What could he possibly have meant by thinking
"My life doesn't mean anything"?

David grew up near Washington, DC, and went to
Catholic grade school. "I believed that Jesus was the Son

of God, but I did not know Him. In fact, I did not know that you *could* know Him, and I knew nothing about the Bible." By the time he was a teenager, David "no longer participated in the Catholic Church."

When David became interested in theater, he acted in several plays. His talent, interest, and dedication to further develop his skills led him to complete his MA in theater at the University of Maryland and his PhD in theater studies from Wayne State University. David spent the next two-plus decades teaching theater at the college and university level, with his final stop being Fordham University at Lincoln Center in New York City.

"For eighteen years, I was the chairman of the Division of Arts of Fordham University at Lincoln Center, New York City. I also continued in my acting career on Broadway, off-Broadway, and on TV."

As good an opportunity as the New York theater community provided for him to use his acting talent and skills, it turned out that there was an even greater purpose for his being there. One night at the very height of his acting career, David was overwhelmed by the sense that his life didn't mean anything. "I started to cry, and I knew I was lost."

David began his search for God by going to several different churches. After some time, an actor friend of his told him about a fellowship of actors, dancers, singers, and models who met in a recording studio in Times Square. He invited David to a meeting. They walked through the darkness and degradation of 41st Street, then nicknamed "Crack Alley."

"My friend led me up some stairs to an upper room, where a meeting was in session. People of different races were singing about Jesus. The worship was beautiful, wonderful. As I stood there, all of a sudden I could not stand up and fell on my knees. It was like a hand had come upon me. I could not stop weeping. Then I met Jesus. I poured out my heart to Him and asked Him to forgive me for my sinful life. To my amazement, He forgave me! It was like a huge weight was lifted off me! As I finally stumbled into a chair, I looked around the room at the worshipping brothers and sisters, and I knew I had come home. I had a new family of African Americans, Jews, Gentiles, and Asians. It was overwhelming. My whole life changed. I started going to all the meetings there. I devoured the Bible. I felt robbed because no one had told me it was God's Word. The words of Jesus imparted life to my hungry heart."

That night, David found the Christ who had been waiting patiently for him to open the door and let Him in. Now he was going to use the brilliant mind that memorized the Shakespearean roles of both Othello and Iago...the energy of an athlete...and the talent of an actor...to serve the Kingdom of Heaven. And God was going to provide a special source of help in this work.

"I fell in love with Karen, a young lady on the worship team in the fellowship whom I met in the recording studio, and we were soon married. Karen is Jewish, and I am not. We began to realize that we were examples of the 'one new man' of Jew and Gentile referred to in Ephesians 2:15 and 2:22, 'being built together for a dwelling place for God in the Spirit.'"

The search for the right church ended when David and Karen walked into Times Square Church. God had called David Wilkerson, minister and author of *The Cross and the Switchblade*, to leave his small-town ministry in Pennsylvania to work with the gangs of New York. Karen worked in Pastor Wilkerson's office and sang with the worship team. David began doing street evangelism. Eventually, he was ordained a minister of the Gospel with World Challenge Ministries' fellowship "in the magnificent Mark Hellinger Theater, where I had attended the Broadway Tony Awards some years earlier." The theater of yesteryear was now the home of Wilkerson's Times Square Church.

"I no longer had any desire to train aspiring actors or teach theater history. I now had a burning passion to share the Gospel with the lost. So I resigned my position as a tenured full professor at Fordham University."

When David first found the Lord, he went to Israel for two weeks. While he was in the Christian quarter of Jerusalem, an Arab woman asked David to pray for her to heal from breast cancer. He did. The next day, a Christian nurse called him to tell him the woman was healed. That healing later led to an event in David's life that, at the time, he never could have anticipated. It happened on David and Karen's first trip to Israel together.

"As my Jewish wife saw the Land of Israel for the first time, she began to weep. She said, 'I've come home!'"

They had lunch with the Arab woman who had been healed on the earlier trip. She told them about the drug epidemic among the Jews and Arabs in the Old City, close to where Jesus was crucified.

"Then my friend looked at me and said, 'David, can you bring your ministry here?' It was a 'Macedonian call' like the man from Macedonia who appeared to the apostle Paul and pleaded with him, saying, 'Come over and help us.'"

David and Karen knew they had heard the call of the Lord through their Arab friend. They began to realize that God was calling them to raise up a rehabilitation center for both Arabs and Jews, as a testimony of the "one new man."

"After praying and preparing for a year, we left everything and moved to Israel in 1989. Many of my theater friends and former students did not understand. But when you hear the call of God, you must obey; otherwise you will miss the destiny He has prepared for you."

Today David is the founder and senior pastor of Carmel Congregation and has oversight of various ministries to Jews and Arabs at different locations in Haifa on Mount Carmel. David and Karen also founded House of Victory in 1991, the first Bible-based residential rehabilitation center for Jews and Arabs in Israel. In addition, they have helped plant three other congregations for Jews, Arabs, and Lebanese. They have a thriving food and clothing distribution center ("Elijah's Cloak") in downtown Haifa.

Carmel Congregation has built a worship center on the highest point of Mount Carmel, on land donated by the Anglican Church's Ministry Among Jewish People. On the same property, they now house a women's shelter for African refugees, mostly single mothers, their children, and orphans from Sudan and Eritrea. "We have survived three wars, including missiles from Saddam Hussein and Hezbollah."

The congregation produces and performs musical productions of biblical feasts such as Passover, Purim, and Ruth. So David still has his hand in theater, but it's now for God's glory.

"It's amazing and humbling to serve the Lord in Israel in these prophetic days. More Jews and Arabs have come to the Lord in the past twenty years than any time since the Book of Acts!"

David Davis…from the heart of entertainment to the heart of God.

2

BILL JANCEWICZ
A Second Language
Bible Translator and Missionary

*Let your moderation be known unto all men. The
Lord is at hand. Be careful for nothing; but in
everything by prayer and supplication with
thanksgiving let your requests be made known unto
God.*

Philippians 4:5–6

When Bill Jancewicz first memorized the verse above as a
teenager, he had no idea that one day he would be making
it accessible to generations of readers who otherwise may
never have seen it in their own language.

Bill had a typically normal childhood for a Catholic boy
raised in Norwich, Connecticut. He attended parochial
school for his early education and then moved on to public
school for his secondary years.

"I had an early natural talent and interest in art, and in
my first couple of years of high school, I studied fine arts.
However, for practical reasons I shifted my focus for the
second half of my high school years to technical studies—
drafting and engineering."

Unknown to Bill, that "practical shift" was the
beginning of the Lord leading him into His work. It
became more evident with another "shift" that happened
about the same time.

"In my last year of high school, some of my friends were Christ-following teens and part of a church youth group at a local Christian and Missionary Alliance church. At their invitation, I attended a youth gathering around Halloween in 1972, where I heard the Gospel for the first time, realized I was a sinner, and responded to the invitation to become a follower of Christ."

It was while attending these youth meetings that Bill met a young woman named Norma Jean, who had also come to know the Lord through the witness of other members of the group. Interestingly, she also found strength in, and memorized, the same passage that Bill had committed to memory earlier. After high school, Bill pursued his studies in machine design and technical drawing and graduated with a two-year degree in engineering.

As for Norma Jean, "We dated briefly but then went our separate ways. Norma Jean moved with her family to Florida; I stayed and worked in my engineering career in Connecticut. Living in a manufacturing region, I felt that I could make a living doing this. The fine-arts field, on the other hand, was far too competitive and uncertain in terms of a paying career."

After spending a year working with a charitable organization that trained disabled persons to enter the workforce, Bill took an entry-level job with a small start-up engineering firm involved in undersea vehicle design and construction. The job gave Bill a chance to do use his engineering training as well as his art talent as a technical illustrator. "I enjoyed the creative part of engineering that technical illustration provided. I was doing 'art' along with the precision and discipline of engineering studies."

By now, Bill had found a home church and was actively involved. The church was part of a denominational mission organization and placed a strong emphasis on missions. It held annual missions conferences, where Bill became increasingly familiar with visiting missionaries and their work. At the same time, he was being mentored by several of the older people in the church, and they were encouraging him to consider a life in vocational Christian service. "One challenge I particularly remember was from a woman at the church who asked me, 'What are you doing with your life that has lasting or eternal value?'"

The question did not escape Bill.

"I considered the path I was on and recalled that all of the work I was doing was mainly concerned with the physical world, things that eventually would rust and decay, no matter how well they were engineered. I also considered that the Bible says that only two things are eternal: the Word of God and the souls of people. I decided then that I would spend my life working with these eternal things."

It was about this time that Bill became acquainted with the work of Wycliffe Bible Translators. He was moved to write to their headquarters and ask them for advice about joining them in their work. Unbeknownst to Bill, the Lord was also placing Wycliffe on the heart of Norma Jean, the friend from many years earlier with whom he had had no recent contact.

Now, Bill was an artist and engineer, not a linguist. What service could he provide to an organization specializing in translations? Of course, God had a master plan.

"I didn't begin to be drawn to service with Wycliffe because of an interest in languages or being a translator. That would have scared me away. No, it was the fact that the Word of God is normally a printed book, and my training was in graphic arts. I initially considered service with Wycliffe as a support person, using my training and skills in engineering and technical drawing to help in the task of physically formatting, illustrating, and printing the translated scriptures."

Bill followed God's call and joined Wycliffe, leaving his engineering career behind. He began with a job providing technical support to the production of translated materials. In 1979, he started additional training at the Moody Bible Institute in Chicago, Illinois. It was at that time that the Lord reconnected Bill with Norma Jean, then a student in primary and elementary education at Bryan College in Tennessee. The two began to write to each other and realized that the Lord was calling them both to serve with Wycliffe. "We saw that our service to the Lord in Wycliffe would be more effective together than separate. We were engaged at the end of 1980 and married in August 1981."

Committed to serve the Lord through work with Wycliffe, Bill and Norma Jean attended Wycliffe's Summer Institute of Language (SIL) at the University of Washington, where they trained in linguistics in 1982 and 1984. The first year, Norma Jean took classes while Bill served as a teaching assistant. The second year, Bill took classes while Norma Jean served on the SIL staff. During that year, they were accepted as members-in-training with Wycliffe.

"We were expecting to serve in a support role, but then our Wycliffe field administrators asked us to consider working in the Naskapi language project working on Bible translation rather than in a support role."

The Naskapi are indigenous inhabitants of eastern Quebec and Labrador, Canada. Their name is translated as "people beyond the horizon," an indication of their remote geographical distance from "mainstream society." The Naskapi language, which is closely related to Cree, is a syllabic script that was first written down in 1840 by a Methodist missionary named James Evans.

"When we arrived in the community, the Naskapi read books that were printed in Cree, but there was no way to reproduce their own language. Computers were just coming into the village. I brought one of the first in 1988, and I designed a system whereby users could type using a standard keyboard to get the syllabic symbols. I drew the characters, calculated the digital outlines, and tested the script with Naskapi readers and writers. Over the years, I improved the system so that now Windows and Macintosh computers can print the language using a high-quality font to produce Naskapi materials. Dozens of Naskapi people type this way now on their own computers, and the font and keyboard program I developed is the one that was used when the Naskapi New Testament was published."

Today, Bill and Norma Jean continue their work in making the full Bible available to the Naskapi in their own language and teaching them about the richness of God's Word and His blessings. "A key element in our lives is our marriage and teamwork and our calling to serve the Lord in missions together."

Philippians 4:5 is a special passage for the Jancewicz couple. Because they followed God's call, today, the Naskapi can read their own special passages…in their own language.

3

CAROL DYCHES LOWE
First the Fire
On-Site Facility Manager, Providence House

And lo, the Lord passed by. There was a great and mighty wind, splitting mountains and shattering rocks by the power of the Lord; but the Lord was not in the wind. After the wind—an earthquake; but the Lord was not in the earthquake. After the earthquake—fire; but the Lord was not in the fire. And after the fire—a soft murmuring sound. When Elijah heard it, he wrapped his mantle about his face and went out and stood at the entrance of the cave.
1 Kings 19:11b–13a

Carol Lowe has good reason to have provided this passage from 1 Kings as the scripture verse to begin her chapter.

The eldest of seven children, Carol was born into a pioneering family of storekeepers and farmers in the then-sleepy, seasonal town of Naples, Florida.

"My paternal grandmother was the moving force behind Naples's first Methodist church. My mother was a staunch Catholic who attended the nearest church, which was a mere forty miles away in Fort Myers. My childhood was basically cradle-Catholic, with a lot of weekly Methodist fellowship and annual summer Vacation Bible Schools at First Baptist. Ecumenical, to say the least, in the 1940s."

At the beginning of Carol's sophomore year in high school, the religious pinball stopped as Carol was enrolled in the Holy Name Academy, a semi-cloistered Benedictine Convent boarding school. What appeared to be a dreaded moment in a young girl's life had just the opposite effect.

"I came to love the structure of that monastic life with its Benedictine Order to the day and season. I especially developed a love for Divine Office, which the nuns chanted in Latin at the appropriate hours. As live-in academy students, we could join in chanting with Mother Superior's permission. I gained that coveted permission early on and spent three academic years studying and learning Gregorian chant, Latin, and sacred music, in addition to a full schedule of classic college prep courses."

Under the watchful eye, and with the guidance and mentoring, of the Mother Superior, Sr. Mary Grace, Carol grew in her appreciation of the community life.

"Throughout my senior year, I thought long and carefully about joining the Order. That spring, in addition to being fitted for a graduation cap and gown, I was also fitted for my postulant habit. If happiness is the quiet certainty that the facets of your life are in total harmony, then that period of time was the happiest in my life." At age seventeen, Carol accepted God's call to His service. But then a string of events made her wonder if God actually declined her offer.

At graduation, Carol found out that she would not be entering the convent. Carol's parents had divorced, and her mother needed Carol's help with her six siblings. Furthermore, her mother had found a husband-to-be for her. A year later, Carol was married. "My 'yes' was not without reservations, but one of a dutiful daughter."

Carol and her new husband settled into the life their parents expected them to lead. They began a family, worked at their respective jobs, and did some community-service work. Then, when Carol was twenty-two, and shortly after the birth of her third child, her mother died.

At the reading of the will, which her mother had written before Carol's high school graduation, she found out that her mother had named Carol and her husband guardians of Carol's siblings. "Obviously, the God who I thought had spurned my vocation to the religious life, along with my mother, had set my life path at a much earlier date. So I said a reluctant 'yes' again."

Over the next decade, Carol and her husband raised ten children while pursuing their jobs.

"In the busyness of everyday life, my personal practice of faith became sporadic, then almost nonexistent. Weekend outings as a family began to replace church attendance. As my job began to consume more than forty hours a week, my personal prayer life became an arid desert. The all-consuming secular life left no time for a meaningful relationship with God. We didn't deny God so much as we ignored Him."

Barely into the second decade of their marriage, Carol's husband ended it. Suddenly single, with five children still at home, Carol felt anger at God. She also felt something else. "Most strangely, I remember wanting to return to a cloistered life, free of worldly distraction, and thinking I might still yet have the time to do that after the youngest child had grown." But just the opposite happened.

Based on previous newspaper experience, Carol landed a job at a newspaper, working for an owner she particularly admired for his ethical and moral principles. As the company grew, so did Carol's responsibilities. Now, as the owner's executive and personnel assistant, Carol was traveling and living well. Hardly the cloistered life she had dreamed of.

Just as her youngest child enrolled in the Navy, Carol's company moved its headquarters to California. Free to move, she relocated with it. "The pay was great, the perks even better. I had even begun to attend daily Mass again. Spiritual growth and counseling were available less than two miles down the road at a Carmelite monastery, and I was living in the middle of Napa Valley with all the cultural life I could ever want less than forty-five minutes away, in San Francisco." All seemed right with the world.

But one day, "the small quiet murmuring once again began in my heart and my head. I just knew I had to return to Naples. I did know that I had come to trust that murmur when I heard it, and when I've become calm in my soul, to act on it. I returned to Naples, not knowing what I was going to do there, or how I was going to afford to do it."

Back in Naples, Carol found part-time, minimum-wage work doing data entry. She also volunteered as a court-appointed Guardian Ad Litem (GAL) for children of families in dependency court. In time, that turned into a paid position in the GAL office. "During the sixteen years I worked there, I came to the realization that it was just about impossible for a single mother to maintain a household, be a single parent, jump through all the hoops the court system required, and find the resources that would help her become self-sufficient. In a kinder, smaller, less complex Naples, I had been there and had done that. I knew I wanted to continue helping these mothers even when my career at GAL ended."

On her return to Naples, Carol also became active in her old parish, which by now had bought her family homestead and turned it into a playground for children. "How pleased Mother must be to see that." Through the church, she met and became friends with a couple who had a vision they called Providence House, which provided living quarters and a safe haven for at-risk women and children.

"I recognized their vision as the same one I had developed while working in the court system. I began to attend their board meetings but was still not 'hands-on' enough. Once the property was purchased and rehabilitation of the apartments had begun, the physical labor I was doing to help brought calm to my heart and peace at the end of the day. I knew I finally had an answer to my question to God: 'God what am I supposed to be doing while I wait in joyful hope for the coming of our Savior?'"

On April 14, 2008, God answered the question. Carol returned home after a day of rehabilitating at the Providence House to find the fire department rolling up their hoses after extinguishing a fire that completely gutted her home. "And that evening, the still, small voice said to me, 'See? I took care of all the worry you had about sorting, packing, and moving. You need nothing except what I give you. You are loved and will want for nothing. I have given you talents and skills beyond measure. Now you are free to do my work.'"

So Carol Lowe moved into Providence House and, using the executive skills she had developed in her corporate career and the lessons she learned in her time with GAL, became the on-site facility manager, aiding the women living there.

"I used to say, 'Someday when the kids are grown and gone, I'm finally gonna join a convent.' One recent quiet evening while sitting on my back porch, gazing at our rock grotto with its eight-foot-high simple wooden cross, the still, small voice had a few more words for me: 'What is a convent but a group of women living in community with a common purpose: to worship God and follow Christ in service to others? Are you not doing that right now?'"

First the wind, then the earthquake, then the fire. Then a soft, murmuring sound.

4

REV. RON MCKEON
An Instrument of God
Anglican Priest and Missionary
CFO for the Anglican Church in North America

> *And we know that for those who love God all things*
> *work together for good, for those who are called*
> *according to his purpose.*
>
> *Romans 8:28*

Ron McKeon's growing years and his education prepared him for many things, including multiple career options. What they did not prepare him for was the unique, almost unspeakable, way that all the preparation would seem pointless right at the time God was calling him to use it.

Ron grew up in one of the first homes built in Levittown, New York, the model for track housing in America. He was the middle child of three boys born to loving parents who shared their own sense of God's importance, each in his and her own way. "Mother saw to it that we attended mass and CCD (Confraternity of Christian Doctrine) classes at the Roman Catholic Church. My father, who did not attend church, reinforced what I learned at church about God our Creator on Sunday afternoons by piling us in the family car for a drive to a park, where we would picnic and enjoy God's creation together as a family."

His parents' religious overtures took hold enough that

by junior high school, Ron felt that he was either supposed to be a priest or get married and have children. "In a short conversation with God, I left it up to Him." God had other ideas. And they began with music. During his high school years, Ron blossomed as a musician. He played sax and clarinet. He sang in the choir and in musicals with a voice strong enough to enter aria competitions.

So accomplished was young Ron that he decided to become a professional musician. But his dad insisted on college. Reluctantly, Ron enrolled at Virginia Commonwealth University, where he performed in ensembles and sang with the Cathedral Choir of the Roman Catholic Diocese. And that was where he met Debby, the girl who was to become his wife and "lifelong helpmate on my journey with my Lord and Savior."

After only a year in college, Ron joined the Marine Corps. And though his dad may not have seen it, the Marines knew a musician when they saw one. Ron spent his active-duty years with the Marines as a professional musician stationed with a variety of combat troops. He also used his time in the service to begin night school, studying business administration. Following the advice of a friend who said, "Whatever field you choose, learn as much as you can about computers," Ron earned both a bachelor's degree and an MBA with a major in information systems.

It was also during this time in the Marines that Ron and Debby joined a family Bible study with some friends. While his Roman Catholic upbringing had given him a very strong knowledge of God and Jesus Christ, it was through these group meetings that Ron was first introduced to the Holy Spirit and came to understand a personal relationship with Jesus. "This experience changed my life forever and helped Debby and me understand that our first vocation was to 'the five gifts on loan from God,' our five daughters." Still, there was the income-generating vocation to consider. So, armed with military experience, an impressive résumé as a musician, and an MBA in information systems, Ron found his "first calling."

"My first career centered on small business and nonprofit administration." His initial job was as a business/computer analyst for a company that manufactured high-purity chemicals and electronic process control equipment. "I reported directly to the VP of Operations. My main responsibility was being the troubleshooter, to propose solutions for any problem identified by the management committee." Over the better part of a decade, Ron's business and solution-minded acumen was used in the wholesale/retail nursery business and in church administration on the West Coast.

When Ron's father passed away unexpectedly, Ron and Debby moved their daughters to Virginia so he could pursue a career closer to their extended family. It was 1988 and the beginning of life changes Ron had never anticipated, beginning with joining a local Episcopal church. He and Debby became fully engaged with their church life, so much so that Ron signed up for a parish-sponsored Education for Ministry seminar. During his four years of study with this program, Ron began to sense that God may be calling him to the Episcopal priesthood.

Over the next fourteen years, while he continued to work in the corporate world as an executive in varying businesses, Ron and Debby wrestled with the feeling that perhaps God had another purpose for his life. Then one weekend, God made Himself clear. On a Cursillo retreat, "I clearly heard the Lord telling me it was time to seek mentorship for a new spiritual direction. While I knew deep down that I was to become equipped for vocational ordained ministry, my understanding of God's call at that point in my life was simply to become equipped to be sent wherever God desired." It took another year before Ron acted. Then, with Debby's full support, he visited Trinity School for the Ministry. Now the call was perfectly clear, and Ron committed to it. He enrolled in seminary.

The ordained ministry seemed to be what a life of preparation in music, leadership, business education, corporate experience, and making presentations had prepared Ron for. This was where God intended to bring it all together.

Then, less than six weeks into his studies, Ron McKeon was diagnosed with terminal stage 4 cancer of the tongue. "My tongue and all of the lymph nodes in my neck would need to be surgically removed immediately. And that was to be followed by chemotherapy and radiation. The surgery left me without a tongue and with a disfigured face."

A person of lesser faith might have decided, at this point, that maybe he really wasn't called after all. Not Ron. He continued online divinity studies, even in his suddenly changed condition. But it wasn't easy.

One night, depressed, nauseated, and weak, Ron logged on to his computer to find a message from a professor friend. It read simply, "Ron, you are awesome."

"I immediately began to weep. The feeling I was experiencing was both like a slap on my face as well as the gentle hand of a friend on my shoulder. At that moment, I felt the Holy Spirit say, 'Don't you realize that I love you more than you love even yourself, and I love you now just as I loved you while I knit you together in your mother's womb? You are my handiwork. You are carefully and wonderfully made because I love you.' It no longer mattered to me whether I would ever be able preach the Gospel with my mouth or remain on a food tube the rest of my life because God loved me. I was His handiwork, and I was created for His unique purpose. That night I completely surrendered myself into the arms of my Lord, Savior, and friend, Jesus Christ."

Reassured and renewed, Ron now knew that God had called him to vocational ministry. In 2007, he finished his Master of Divinity degree. And, through Marine perseverance and with the help of his family and the Lord,

Ron taught himself to speak again so that he could preach.

"I do believe my first careers were a part of my calling, even though I was not aware of it at the time. One of my favorite Bible passages is Psalm 139:16: 'Your eyes saw my unformed substance; in your book were written, every one of them, the days that were formed for me, when as yet there was none of them.' The common thread throughout my pastoral and missionary service is the gift of administration honed by my musical training and education in computer programming and business-analysis experience. They all are being used to the glory of the Lord."

Today, Ron is in the vocational service of the Lord as pastor, missionary, and church executive. And, while he may not be playing his saxophone much, he is a virtuoso at trumpeting the love of God.

5

CATHERINE KAPIKIAN
A Sacred Pallet
Artist, Teacher, and Author

*And the peace of God, which passes all
understanding, shall keep your hearts and minds
through Christ Jesus.*

Philippians 4:7

"Ever since I can remember, I thought of myself as an artist. I don't know how to be anything else, nor did I want to be anything else."

God knew how Catherine Kapikian felt about being an artist. After all, He gave her the talent. That's why He never asked her give up her love of art for work in His service. He simply asked that she redirect her talent—and her life.

As a child, Catherine was surrounded by a family who appreciated her talent. Her two brothers shared their model-building interest with their sister. She designed, built—from scratch—and painted models of anything from stagecoaches to boats. Her parents recognized and encouraged her budding artistic talent. "My aptitude for transcending materials grew, and so did my enthrallment. And when I copied a picture of a princess three times its original size, in comparable format, my mother complimented me so extravagantly that it galvanized a way of thinking about shifting scales—a skill I use to this day in my commissioned work."

Catherine had another compelling interest during her growing years in Palm Beach, Florida: Bethesda by the Sea Episcopal Church. She spent as much time as she could around its formal gardens and in its sanctuary. "My head and heart dwelled in this lofty and shimmering place. In a space where shrouded mysteries and beauty pierced my poetic being, the radiance of sun-drenched, colored windows coupled with the enormity of dazzling sound, conspired in worship to conjure up within me a notion that God was real. To this day, I remember leaving the church with the words, 'May the peace of God which passes all understanding…' echoing in my heart and sustaining my soul. God has remained real ever since."

Raised in a family in which almost every male was a physician, Catherine knew about medicine. So, as she began to think about a career in art, it was a natural progression for her talent to go from broad strokes of interest to the finite area of medical art. She began her formal education at the Carnegie Mellon School of Fine Arts, transferring before her junior year to the University of Pennsylvania. During the summer between the two schools, Catherine spent time as an intern in the medical illustration department at the National Institutes of Health (NIH). In February of the next year, now married and delaying her education, she returned to NIH as a vocational medical illustrator.

"I loved the mixture of cognitive discipline and imaginative thinking required to give image to medical information in the context of its use—for instance, a table exhibit on cystic fibrosis. I also valued the fact that I was bringing my artistic skills to bear within a community in which the members worked on behalf of the good."

With the birth of her first son, Catherine elected to become a vocational homemaker. It was a twelve-year hiatus from work, but not art. She used those years to complete her college education. Maybe now she would return to her career as a medical illustrator.

Then, in her early thirties, on a Christmas Eve, Catherine required emergency surgery. During her stay in the hospital, a Navy chaplain visited her. "I didn't like him initially, so out of guilt, after I returned home and convalesced, I invited him to dinner. He looked around at the artwork and said, 'The next time you return for your neurosurgical appointment, stop by the chaplains' office. We've been talking about acquiring some paraments— symbolic table coverings of faith in the alter area in for the chapel.'" Catherine did stop by and was commissioned to create a set of Pentecost fronts that required use of both her artistic and sewing skills. Her work was so well received that she was commissioned to create a set of six large, complex wall hangings for the liturgical seasons. As Catherine worked on the sacred art, she had a realization: "I discovered I knew nothing about theology."

So, at age thirty-five, Catherine Kapikian enrolled in Wesley Theological Seminary and spent the next four years earning a Master of Theological Studies degree. But she never put away her brushes—at least not intellectually. "By graduation time, I had discerned that theological education as I had experienced it without the arts was truncated, and that seminary education nationwide was arid as well in this respect."

Catherine presented the seminary with a proposal to create a position for an artist-in-residence. After initially rejecting the idea, the seminary reversed its position and offered her an adjunct teaching job, the title of artist-in-residence, and a basement classroom to use as a studio. "That spring I heard more than once the parable of the mustard seed in chapel worship and Sunday services. I thought a lot about that parable during that time and wondered if its message of unconditional trust could possibly apply to me. One day, hard at work with my new undertaking, I said, 'Yes, why not?' And then it dawned on me that I had a ministry on my hands."

Catherine was right. And her life in the seminary community proved it to her day after day. "I knew of the richness, joy, and revelatory power the arts bring to living. I knew that the arts communicate truths suggestively and obliquely in ways that words never could. I knew that art and religion were siblings because they both articulate purpose and meaning in life. And there I was—right in the middle of a seminary—a logical place for theology and art to meet face to face, learn from one another, and each do their work better because of the other."

Catherine has another reason she is certain God called her to a ministry in sacred art: "Landing a great big, messy working studio with multiple artists-in-residence and later a jewel-like, museum-quality gallery, all the while lacking the 'essential PhD'…right in the middle of academia! How improbable otherwise?"

Much of the artwork Catherine has produced over her years of Christian service is for hospital interfaith chapels. It is a context she particularly loves to work in. She attributes much of that to her time at NIH and the interaction with the doctors there. It gave her an additional glimpse into the daily challenges a patient faces and an empathy that enables her to bring something special to hospital chapels.

"Furthermore, the complexity of juggling much information with imaginative cogitation in medical illustration was not unlike what I do now when I juggle all the disparate information related to a specific site—a church chancel, for instance—with an imaginative solution."

When Catherine was a young mother, she dreamed of creating artwork for churches but didn't have a clue how to do that. God did. And when He called her, He filled in the "how." Recently, Catherine retired as director of the Henry Luce III Center for the Arts and Religion, which she founded. Although she no longer has administrative and faculty responsibilities at Wesley Theological

Seminary, she continues to teach there as a Distinguished Artist-in-Residence. And she is still creating large-scale works for religious spaces on a commission basis.

"The past thirty years have been extraordinary. Filled with exciting commissions in religious spaces all over the country, speaking and teaching engagements in and outside of this country, writing numerous articles, and a book titled *Art in Service of the Sacred*. I'm still keeping a steady march toward the integration of the arts into theological education. It's all based on the premises I developed that yielded a prototype model for theological education at large. What a great blessing and privilege! It is hard to tell the difference, and I don't think I want to, between my life and my art. Amen."

Ever since Catherine can remember, she has thought of herself as an artist. So has God.

6

SR. ANNE GUINAN
Elsie Out, God In
Video Producer, Mission Helpers of the Sacred Heart

*I give you a new commandment: love one another,
such as my love has been for you, so must your love be
for each other.*

John 13:34

Sister Anne Guinan can trace the beginnings of her life of Christian service back to her home life and days in a Catholic elementary school. "Surely that was the basis for my life—a simple relationship with Jesus and His love for people." Shortly after Anne was confirmed, the family relocated, and Anne's Catholic schooling ended. With that, what seemed a straight line to religious life turned into a giant curve.

Anne maintained her close relationship with Jesus through her teen years, which usually included daily Mass during Advent and Lent and other church activities. However, as time passed, she found her perspective on her relationship with Jesus changing from the broad understanding she had learned as a youngster. "I guess it turned into more of a 'Jesus and me' mentality." A short-lived interest in the Newman Club at the University of Michigan reinforced her now-narrowed faith walk, one that seemed fine for the moment.

With college classes and a career path to worry about,

Anne left ponderings on eternal matters for later and turned her attention to more temporal, but immediate, matters. Her life was full. There were turns at engineering for designing sailboats, studying French, flying lessons that she rode to on a motorcycle, dating, even weighing marriage. And, finally, graduating with a degree in French and beginning a career.

Her first job was as a secretary at one of the largest advertising agencies in the world, Young & Rubicam. The fast-paced atmosphere of the Manhattan-based agency suited Anne. Soon she was promoted to traffic manager, ensuring that clients' ads were finished on schedule and into the hands of the media outlets that would run them. It was a critical and demanding role in the ad-agency business, and heady work for a young woman. Her ascendancy put her in the right crowd in the right business. But, with all of that, she could not escape the recurring question, "What are you doing with your life?"

The sense that she should be doing "something for God" outweighed the urge to do something for advertisers. "Somehow," she recalls, "Elsie the Borden Talking Cow and No More Tears baby shampoo just didn't seem important."

At twenty-eight, the signs that she was not where God wanted her were becoming more evident. Anne had taken graduate courses in philosophy and theology in an effort to know God in a deeper way. They were stimulating intellectual pursuits, but not life changing. On a retreat for young career women, she found the talk of business and careers strangely alien. At routine cocktail parties with other young professionals, where once she had been comfortable, Anne felt out of place. "I felt strongly that this was not where I belonged. God was giving me a message."

One afternoon while riding the train to Long Island for the weekend, Anne began reading a book on spirituality. Although the title of the book has since escaped her, the message at the time did not. "It was there sitting on that train that I knew, without a doubt, that the Lord was calling me to serve Him in some special way."

Now needing to find out exactly how and where He wanted her, Anne began to explore her options. Browsing bookstores, she found herself drawn to books about Catholic religious orders. She recalled with fondness her school years with the Sisters of the Sacred Heart, so she visited some Dominican Sisters who ran a school in New York City. She had always been impressed with St. Dominic's concern for the poor. Although she didn't feel called to teaching, which was one of their main ministries, she decided she had to do something. She was accepted into a Dominican congregation in Ohio.

Then God intervened again. When Anne told her widowed father what she was going to do, he asked her if she would first take an aunt on a European tour. She agreed. While booking the trip, she found out that a priest was leading a tour on that ship. Pleased to add a spiritual dimension to the vacation, she and her aunt joined the tour. One night over dinner, several fellow travelers talked glowingly about a group of Sisters in New York and their special work with the poor. There it was, the basic lesson from her childhood: a simple relationship with Jesus and His love for the poor. Anne knew what she was hearing. "This is God giving me a message."

Anne learned that the Order discussed at that dinner was the Mission Helpers of the Sacred Heart. When Anne returned to the States, she contacted the Order and followed up with a visit to its New York convent. When she saw the work they were doing with the poor, Anne knew that the question that had haunted her earlier years—"What are you doing with your life?"—could be best answered by serving God with the Mission Helpers.

In 1955, on an autumn Sunday in New York when churches across America were celebrating the Feast of Christ the King, former advertising executive Anne

Guinan joined the Mission Helpers and became Sister Anne Guinan. "For me, God was in all those experiences I had, knocking me on the head and trying to get me going in the right direction. I've found that my background in the real world was good preparation for religious life. All the personal relationships, planning, strategies, and meeting deadlines became important tools in teaching religion, setting up diocesan programs, and even in editing our *Mission Helper* magazine for a number of years."

Sr. Anne had put her life in advertising behind her…or so she thought. But the Lord had other ideas. Sr. Anne was to put her Madison Avenue experience to work again. Only this time, it wasn't selling milk and shampoo. She would be marketing God's love through the production of video programs. Nearly thirty years after leaving the media world, Sr. Anne joined with Sr. Caritas Kennedy to form Mission Helper Productions. Working together, doing their own writing, camera work, and editing, they have produced scores of video programs promoting the Lord's work for a variety of organizations and causes, across the country and internationally. Much of their work has been centered on the lives of Christians in the Holy Land.

For Sr. Anne Guinan, the straight line to Christian service became a curve that has turned into a full circle.

7

DEDI WHITAKER
An Answer for Peggy Lee
Youth Worker and Church Administrator

But this I call to mind, and therefore I have hope:
The steadfast love of the Lord never ceases, his
mercies never come to an end; they are new every
morning; great is your faithfulness.

Lamentations 3:21–23

Dedi Whitaker experienced a reservation about God's calling that's not unusual among new Christians. "I was fearful in my early days as a Christian that He would call me to a place far away as a missionary, which scared me to death." God didn't. He had work for her to do in her own community.

Things between God and Dedi got rocky early. Her father was a very religious man who saw to it that his children attended church, even though that meant driving from New Jersey into New York City just to get to an Anglo–Catholic church. His reward for their patience was breakfast at the Automat, and that was just fine with Dedi and her siblings. They loved their dad, and his treat-topped trips were fine with them. Then things changed.

"When I was twelve, my father died suddenly of peritonitis poisoning, despite my fervent prayers and many promises to God to 'behave' if He would heal my Daddy. I decided that God was either a figment of the imagination like Santa Claus, or just so spiritual that he wasn't really involved in our lives. I pretty much left Him alone from then on."

The remaining family moved to Baltimore, where Dedi attended a college prep school on a scholarship. But the money was not there for her to go college. "This left me with an inferiority complex, as I was literally the only one in my graduating class from high school who did not go to college. I was driven to read voraciously to try and 'keep up' with my friends at Smith, Vassar, and Wellesley. The end result was, I think, a pretty well-rounded education, as well as a desire for knowledge."

After high school graduation, Dedi went to secretarial school and took a job as the secretary for the leasing department of a development company. "In those days, most women in my socioeconomic group worked just to fill time between school and marriage."

In due time, Dedi met Hal, the man who was to become her husband. Hal was a Christian Scientist who practiced his faith beyond Sunday worship. Dedi liked that about him and started attending church with Hal. But she still felt a void. So she started investigating other forms of religion, including theosophy and other monist and New Age ideas. "I was all about intellectual and Gnostic elitism."

Hal and Dedi were married. As soon as Dedi became pregnant, she left her job to become a vocational wife and mother. It was a job she loved, and she still loves it. As happy as she was, Dedi found herself asking, along with the Peggy Lee song of the era, "Is that all there is?" Thus began a renewed quest for "truth."

The truth came from a cousin. He was smart, and she, feeling it was okay to listen to an intellectual, decided to hear what he had to say.

"He shared the Gospel with me—so simple: God loves us and wants to be in a relationship with us, but we want to be our own god, and our sins have created a separation between Him and us. He has solved the problem through His Son, Jesus, who has borne the punishment for our rebellion on our behalf and closed the gap. But we have to personally receive the gift He offers of eternal life and relationship with Him. This cousin challenged me very specifically and said, 'You need to accept Jesus as your Savior. I guarantee you this is the true truth—what we have been looking for our whole lives.'"

That night, Dedi lay awake considering everything her cousin had told her. "I felt as though I were standing on the edge of a swimming pool I was being called to dive into. I had no idea if there was water in it or not. I knew that if I 'dove in' and there was nothing there, it would be the end of my belief in anything. The end of any faith I might have had. I stood there, poised and shivering, and realized that I might never have this opportunity again. So I leapt and invited Jesus to come into my heart. No trumpets, no visions, but just to make sure God knew I meant business, I actually got on my knees by the side of the bed, very carefully so as not to awaken Hal."

Now Dedi had it all—the Lord truly in her life, a loving husband, who soon after also gave his life to Christ, two lovely daughters, and a happy home. She thought she knew what the Lord had planned for her. But the Lord wasn't finished.

The same cousin who led her to the Lord had been volunteering for a youth organization called the Fellowship of Christians in Universities and Schools, or FOCUS. One day he called Dedi and told her that two high school students from Baltimore had been to the FOCUS camp and were coming home filled with excitement about their newfound faith. Her cousin wanted Dedi to help them grow spiritually.

That was it. No lightning bolt, no special moment, no series of signs. And no tug of war with God over His call.

"I was overwhelmed at the prospect. I immediately started a little Bible study with the students. Eventually, with Hal's help, I assembled a group of adults and began a chapter of the FOCUS ministry in Baltimore that continues now, even thirty years later."

For Dedi, the call to God's service did not require, as it often does, folding up her tent and moving to another place in life. No seminary. No move to another part of the world. Not even giving up her lifestyle. "Every calling of God is personally tailor-made to the individual, and God knows exactly the right fit for each person. He even takes into account what you like doing. It's a matter of discerning the calling, which is often a case of 'bloom where you're planted.'" It was for Dedi.

As Dedi looks back at the years preceding her work with young people through her leadership role in FOCUS, she realizes that even the seemingly routine aspects of our lives are often preparation for God's call. "Along with the lessons learned just from working with people, the most important skill acquired from my first career, I believe, was the ability to type well and fast, communicate on paper, and organize my thoughts, and that led me to learn various computer skills." She even sees her career as wife and mother as training her to work with teenagers.

"I don't think any life experience, good or bad, or any natural gift, is ever wasted when it is turned over to God. If ever there were a case of making a 'silk purse out of a sow's ear,' it's what God can do with His messy Christians when they invite Him into their lives to take charge."

As Dedi and Hal entered into their retirement years, Dedi arranged to leave her supervisory role at FOCUS and spend more time with Hal, their children, and their grandchildren. Plus, she had become a founding member of a church plant that needed the leadership qualities that Dedi had honed over her years with FOCUS. Her role in the nurturing of that church became critical to its success, and she enjoyed contributing in whatever way she was led. Life was settling into a well-earned pastoral pattern.

Then, quite suddenly, the Lord called Hal home. And

He called Dedi back into her work with helping young people find God's grace and grow in His love. She resumed a part-time job with FOCUS. He filled the rest of her working time with an expanded role in her growing church, with increased leadership duties as a paid administrator. In this latter role, Dedi has been, and continues to be, a central player in leading the lay work of the new church in its day-to-day activities and growth.

"In my seventy years, I have found life since becoming a Christian to be more fulfilling and richer than I could have imagined. It has provided the strength to live through the 'slings and arrows of outrageous fortune,' as well as a life that is filled with joy—exciting, surprising, and with the promise that it goes on into eternity."

The Lord called Dedi Whitaker to vocational Christian service and used her right where she was. She bloomed where she was planted. And that long-ago fear of being called to be a missionary to a place far away? "He may still call me for that. If He does, I know now it will be exactly what will most fulfill me."

8

REV. DAVID STENNER
A Call in Aisle Five
Episcopal Priest

With man this is impossible, but with God all things are possible.

Matthew 19:26

David Stenner was called early.

"When the bishop laid hands on me at my confirmation at age twelve, I knew then that I was called to vocational service, but I didn't know what that would mean until years later." And he wouldn't heed it immediately, even then. He just wasn't ready yet. He had other things to do first. But God wasn't giving up on David Stenner.

Young David grew up like most boys—school, Little League baseball, neighborhood friends, and his family all played roles in his average, lower-middle-class life. As with many young people at that time, he and his older sister were taken to church by their mother, a devout Roman Catholic. "Dad would come to Mass on Easter and Christmas Eve, and that was a special experience for me."

Though David was careful that his friends didn't see it, his mother's commitment to a foundation in faith for him was not wasted. "Some of my earliest memories were in church: stained-glass windows, liturgy, and a peaceful sense of awe at the beauty and power of God were etched into my memory from a very early age."

Then in his teen years, those wonderful memories were destroyed, and any desire to pursue the ministry was squelched.

"A verbally abusive priest and the attempted sexual abuse of an usher turned the church from a place of peace and awe to a place of fear and shame. I made every excuse to stay away, but my mother was firm in her commitment to raise her children in the faith. In my later teen years, I finally had my way and refused to go."

Leaving any remaining thoughts of the priesthood far behind him, David zeroed in on one of his other childhood fascinations: sports. Baseball and football. A number of major universities recruited the young athlete to play football. No one in his family had ever been to college. David had hoped to be the first. But low grades denied him that opportunity. "I opted for junior college and again had a very promising athletic future playing professional baseball. God had other ideas, ending my hopes for success with an injury during my final year of football. I was now alone and headed toward a duplication of my parents' lives—find a steady job, raise a family, and get by."

All hopes of sports stardom dashed, David took a job at a local retail chain. Soon he worked his way up to assistant manager. In time, the company moved him to another city and into a management position. Alone and without guidance or social structure, David became part of the late '60s/early '70s free-living lifestyle. In a life far removed from his Catholic upbringing, David had a whole new set of interests. And that was fine with him.

Until one night when David ended up in a revival meeting among a whole group of young people who had come to know Jesus. Something they had appealed to him.

"Over a period of months, my heart began to burn for the peace and awe I had when I was young. During one of the rallies, the speaker called me to the front of the assembly and asked if I wanted Jesus to live in my heart. I immediately responded, 'Yes! *Yes!*' From that day forward, my life was dramatically changed." David's faith grew as he spent time every day in worship, prayer, and Bible study with the other young Christians. And soon God tapped David, much as He had touched him through the bishop years earlier.

"It was during this time that I heard the voice of God calling me to service." But David still wasn't quite ready to accept it.

At twelve, when he had first heard God calling, David was too young to do much about it. This time, there was a career and a family to consider. He was in a good place. Starting at the bottom, David had worked his way up to store manager, supervising more than one hundred employees. His skills with people and management became so refined that the corporation made him a troubleshooter, sending him from store to store to solve personnel problems. He was so convinced that he was where he should be that he returned to college and earned a degree in business management with a focus on personnel development.

"I was doing well financially, supporting my wife and three children with a life that was better than I had as a child." In addition to growing a family and a career, David was also growing in the spirit of the Lord. "I was deeply involved as a lay person in the local congregation, taught Sunday School, was a member of the vestry, was a lay reader, served as a Eucharistic minister, and did whatever else the church needed. The call to full-time ministry was still there, but the demands of life continued to take precedence."

What David came to know later was that God was using the time with his retail job to give him gifts he would use in his service to the Lord. His successful career gave him self-confidence and taught him that any kind of accomplishment was within reach, all of which would come to help him in his ministry. "I also learned the business skills needed to administer a church, the things they don't teach in seminary. Most of all, I grew in my faith and trust in God's grace, provision, and guidance."

Thirteen years had passed since God's second notice to David. And it appeared that He was ready to try again. Only this time, it was going to have a little more of the "Saul on the road to Damascus" feel to it.

"During a prayer meeting, a priest prayed over me and shared a vision that he saw of me being ordained. Needless to say, I felt the hand of God hitting me alongside my head."

But David still wrestled with it. Could he really leave a successful career and return to school? What about his family and their needs? David still wasn't getting it, so God intensified the light—and added a little heat.

"It is marvelous how God works all things for the good for those who love Him and are called to His purpose. About the same time as I was struggling with my call, the company was sold. A year into the new regime, the owner of the company came to my office and gave me notice that my services were no longer needed. Of course, I was devastated and went through a very difficult crisis of faith."

With his job gone, health insurance dropped, and financial resources depleted, David took any odd jobs he could find—painter, construction helper, janitor. "We had to learn to live by the provision that could come only from God."

During this difficult time, David finally responded to God's call and entered the seminary. "The next three years were some of the toughest and best years of our lives. But God provided in every way. In time, I was ordained and assigned to a small rural congregation on the north coast of California. Sundays saw an average attendance of seventeen people. That congregation grew to become a stable, self-sufficient parish in the nine years we served there. From there we moved to my present position, knowing with all of my heart, 'Nothing is impossible with God.'"

David surely knows something else about God and the "impossible": He doesn't give up because we aren't quite ready, no matter how long it takes to get our attention. Fr. David Stenner will be eternally grateful for that.

"I find it both humbling and amazing that He took a kid with no academic history and no social status and allowed me to receive four college degrees and to have the privilege to serve Him as a priest in the one, holy catholic Church. I wake up with a thankful heart every morning."

David Stenner heard God call him as a child and every time after that. It just took David a while to listen and let God do the impossible.

9

KEITH THIBODEAUX
Dance for Jesus
Cofounder, Ballet Magnifcat!

*You are my hiding place; you will deliver me from
trouble and surround me with shouts of deliverance.*
                                          Psalm 32:7

You know Keith Thibodeaux. You couldn't miss getting to
know him.

Whether you first watched television when you could
enjoy it only in black and white or still watch TV in high-
definition (HD) color, you know Keith Thibodeaux.

Keith was born in Lafayette, Louisiana. He was the
oldest of six children brought up in a Roman Catholic
household. The rest of his story might have been about a
boy growing up in a Southern city, a young man playing
drums in a bayou band working in the local bars and
taking bookings for weddings and reunions. If that had
been the rest of the story, you might never have known
who Keith is. But his story is far different than that one.
And that's why you know him. "When I was four years
old, my family moved to Los Angeles." The move to the
mecca of the entertainment industry was a life-changing
event for little Keith. The cute, self-taught, but nonetheless
proficient drummer boy was noticed by one of America's
most popular bands of the swing era. And the future began
to unfold.

"When I was four years old, I played professionally

with Horace Heidt and His Musical Knights." But that's still not why you know Keith.

As many talented children do in Los Angeles, Keith auditioned for television shows. Those auditions are routine events in Hollywood; talent just rushes from one to another. But one casting session was different for the young actor/musician.

"I auditioned for the *I Love Lucy* show producers for the role of the Ricardos' son, Little Ricky." From among hundreds, Keith was chosen for the part. "I was signed to a seven-year contract with Desilu Studios."

That's why you know Keith Thibodeaux, aka Richard Keith. He was the sweet, precocious son of America's favorite couple, Ricky and Lucy Ricardo. Even sour old Fred Mertz liked Little Ricky. As did all of the cast members. "The cast was very nice to me."

If the story had ended there, it would be a nice little nugget of entertainment trivia. But it didn't.

In real life, Lucy and Ricky's marriage dissolved. The Ricardos' subsequent divorce ended the TV series. And Keith's childhood ended, both on the screen and in real life. The real world is not Never-Never Land, and Keith was not Peter Pan. The only role left for Keith was Keith Thibodeaux. The only family he had left was his. And that wasn't going so well.

When Keith was fifteen, his mother and father separated. "That started a spiral of rebellion." And part of that meant pulling away from his parents.

At about the same time his relationship with his parents was unraveling, Keith joined a rock band as its drummer. With no anchor to keep him from drifting, Keith soon coasted into the entertainer lifestyle that has sunk so many lives…sex, drugs, and rock 'n roll.

"When I was twenty-four, I finally came to the end of my rope."

While Keith had been taking a path of destruction, back home in Louisiana his mother was on the road to a deepening relationship with her Lord. Now a member of the Charismatic Catholic Church, she saw an increasing need for a son lost in the excesses of a fallen world to, at the least, be exposed to Christ's salvation. So she invited Keith to join her at church. He went. And Keith's life changed forever.

"At this meeting, I had an encounter with Jesus Christ. And I became a Christian. I had a vision of the Lord Jesus where He appeared to me and showed me that He was the one who died for my sins and was raised for my justification."

The love of the Lord he experienced that night changed his life. That, of course, also changed his perceptions of his talents. He began to understand that they were a gift…a gift from an almighty God. And that God had a plan for the talents He had given Keith.

"I felt that the Lord wanted me to use the musical gift He had given me as a little boy for His Kingdom's purposes. He called me into service, I believe, to fulfill His calling to go to the ends of the world and preach the Gospel through the prophetic words of Psalm 100:49 and 150, which declare that we praise the Lord with music—with instruments and dance."

It would not have been unreasonable to expect that the next line in this story would read, "I left my rock 'n roll band and formed a Christian band." But in Christ, the unexpected is the reasonable. "I witnessed to my rock band and told them that we needed to change the lyrics of our songs to godly ones. They eventually became believers, and we began the Christian rock band David and the Giants." To date, the band has recorded a dozen albums and is one of the nation's most popular contemporary Christian bands.

Psalm 149:3 declares, "Let them praise his name with dancing and make music to him with timbrel and harp." With music and dance. Keith didn't have to look far to fulfill the "dance" factor. Kathy, his wife and business partner, was an accomplished dancer. "Kathy heeded the call to dance for the Lord." God had delivered the whole package—and with it the vision for a broader opportunity to witness. Combining their talents, Keith and Kathy created "Ballet Magnifcat!," a celebration of God's love and salvation in music and dance.

"Both 'Ballet Magnificat!' and 'David and the Giants' are dedicated to presenting the Gospel through our shows, by touring nationally and internationally to churches, theaters, schools…through any venue open to the presentation of the glory of our Lord."

Keith, Kathy, and the rest of the members of the touring family are faithful that God will continue to provide for them and their ministries because "God has always been faithful to us."

"Little Ricky" may be why you knew Keith Thibodeaux before. His love of his Lord and the way he witnesses about his Savior is why you'll remember him now.

The little boy America loved is now the man who loves God.

10
DEENA GRAVES
Psalm 91:1 for Children
Founder, Traffick911

He who dwells in the shelter of the Most High will rest in the shadow of the Almighty.

Psalm 91:1

When God called Deena Graves to join the fight to stop sex trafficking of children in the United States, she couldn't imagine why He chose her. But, as always, God knew.

"I didn't have an easy childhood. I had a highly dysfunctional family and was sexually molested by my brother. While this in no way compares to the brutalization and terror that victims of domestic minor sex trafficking suffer, it allows me some insight into the trauma of sexual abuse. God uses the pains we have suffered to comfort others. Our struggles and trials are never wasted."

Shy and lacking confidence as a child, Deena's inability to make solid friendships was compounded by frequently moving during her growing years. Itinerancy and a series of traumatic events with no one in particular to turn to for help, strength, or hope were taking their toll on Deena.

"The God-sized hole in my heart was a gaping crater. I needed a strong father figure, and only God could give me that."

When she was sixteen, the family moved again.

Another new school, another uphill battle to meet and make new friends. But this time, something would be different. Deena was introduced to a girl who was a leader in a local Christian youth group. She invited Deena to attend church with her. The shy teen in a new town soon found herself involved in the church's activities. One night after a service, Deena, her friend, and the youth minister went to the local Dairy Queen.

"Sitting in the parking lot with the strong smell of onions from the youth minister's cheeseburger, I met my Savior head-on. It was the most amazing experience of my life. That was the night I found hope and strength to face whatever life brings with joy."

A rekindled Deena finished high school, went on to college, and graduated with a degree in journalism and then a master's degree in public relations.

"After graduation, I took a test to tell me what I was suited for. It said undercover CIA agent, preacher, or journalist. Journalist seemed to fit, offering the adventure without the danger of a CIA agent and giving me the opportunity to use writing for God's purposes."

Deena worked for two newspapers before moving into the corporate communications department at Texas Instruments. When she began a family, she left her job and stayed home to raise her children. When she returned to the company eleven years later, it was in the midst of a major transition. Her new job was stressful and required long hours at work, topped by a three-hour commute each day.

"I couldn't understand the ninety-minute drive each way and the complete chaos I walked back into. Just like the Israelis whined and complained in the desert, I spent most of the two years I was making that drive questioning God's purpose for that job. Little did I know that God was preparing me for the most amazing and important adventure of my life—the unique and humbling experience of watching His hand move for the oppressed."

It was during this trying and tiring time that a missionary to Thailand came to speak at her church. "I was tired, emotional, and barely seeing my family, so I decided not to go." But God had other plans for Deena that night. "God has a way of getting you where He wants you, and He had me at that meeting despite my determination to stay home."

The missionary was speaking about sex tourism in Thailand. Deena assumed she was going to talk about her work to help save young women who had made the choice to become prostitutes. "I lived in my own Christian, American bubble and had never heard of human trafficking." But she did that night.

"I walked into an unexpected world that night. A world where young children are bought and sold for the profit and pleasure of others. A world where their own families sell them for survival. A world where their perpetrators don't care how much torture they put the children through. A world where men desire children and go a long way to fulfill that desire. The missionary showed us photos and a video of the young survivors. She told us their stories of abuse, horror, rescue, and survival."

After the service, Deena shared with her pastor her dismay that people in third-world countries could do something so horrible to their own children. The pastor said that a mutual friend in the Dallas Police Department told him that sex trafficking of children was a problem in America too. Deena protested, "No way. We are a civilized, Christian country. We would not do that to our children." That conversation was the beginning of Deena's new journey. She had been called.

"God led me to hours of research where I learned it not only happens in the United States, but we're a leader in both selling and buying children. We grow them ourselves to service the demand. And we're very good at keeping it hidden because so many of the buyers, as well as some of the traffickers, are influential, powerful people. And I learned that because it is a hidden epidemic, very little was being done to help our American children. Most resources were being poured into other countries or into victims brought into our country."

In spite of the horrendous problem that Deena's research had revealed, and despite her personal angst about the sexual exploitation of children in America, Deena had other commitments that had to have a priority in her life. She had children and a demanding job, both needing all the time and attention she could give them.

"From there, I had a battle with God. He kept calling me to help, and I kept telling Him He had the wrong person. I didn't know anything about this crime, and I certainly didn't know anything about starting and running a nonprofit. But I had nightmares. I couldn't sleep. I couldn't eat. The images were forever burned into my mind. I knew something had to be done, but I also knew I wasn't the one to do it. I didn't have a clue of even where to begin. And I wasn't in a position to quit my job. But when God calls you, He equips, and He provides. He led me through a series of events, and He won."

In 2009, Deena Graves left the corporate world behind and, with the help and support of her tiny inner-city church plant, founded Traffick911, an organization guided by Deena's Christian faith with a mission "to end the buying and selling of American children." Traffick911 partners with fellow abolitionists around the world to prevent child sex trade; rescue those who are victims of it; and restore them to a safe, loving, and nurturing place where they can heal.

"The name 'Taffick911' expresses the urgency of this ministry. The average life expectancy of an American child forced into sexual slavery is just seven short years. We don't have time to wait. The '911' also reflects the words of reassurance found in Psalm 91:1."

The communications and journalistic tools God gave Deena during her working years before Traffick911 were instrumental in helping her and her fellow workers raise the issue of sexual slavery in America to a new level internationally when they mounted the very successful "I'm Not Buying It" campaign during the 2011 Super Bowl.

"I have had the joy of seeing more miracles of God since starting this ministry than I've seen in my entire life. It is like in Matthew, where he says the people were struck by awe. On the other side, the amount of spiritual warfare in this ministry is beyond description. These children are kept in cages, starved, beaten, burned, whipped with wire hangers, drugged, and humiliated. We are not on the frontlines. We are down in Satan's camp. We are constantly surrounded by darkness and evil. It is critical to cling to Him to survive seeing this level of depravity in humans."

The journey from a childhood of loneliness, molestation, and uncertainty to founder of an organization to confront the evils of sexual slavery hasn't been an easy one for Deena Graves. But it is one well worth it for Deena and the children she is saving.

"Obedience to God can be so difficult and can bring much pain and suffering, but it is the most amazing experience a person can have on this earth."

11

REV. DION THOMPSON
A New Byline
Episcopal Priest

I appeal to you therefore, brothers and sisters, by the
mercies of God, to present your bodies as a living
sacrifice, holy and acceptable to God, which is your
spiritual worship. Do not be conformed to this world,
but be transformed by the renewing of your minds, so
that you may discern what is the will of God—what
is good and acceptable and perfect.

Romans 12:1–2

"One day I asked the priest, 'Why am I here?' She responded by saying that possibly God was calling me to the priesthood. I laughed. It was a most preposterous idea. A black priest? With dreadlocks? Heck, I wasn't even an Episcopalian."

Dion Thompson was raised in a home filled with the arts. His mother was a poet and writer, and his stepfather was an artist. It was a fascinating childhood that set him on the path for a career as a writer. He majored in English at California State University–Long Beach and subsequently earned an MFA in professional writing and publishing from the University of Southern California. Professionally, then, the road ahead was clear.

Spiritually, things weren't that clear. "I was baptized as a child in the Methodist Church. My most profound childhood memories come from the Pentecostal-style church my grandmother attended. The preaching was fire and brimstone, and it was not unusual for someone to 'get happy' or start speaking in tongues. During my teen years, my mother attended the Christian Science Church. At about sixteen or seventeen, I stopped going to church altogether."

With a writing career fully in sight, Dion made a decision to forgo the great American novel or any attempt at it. "I decided on newspapering. I liked to write. I liked writing about and meeting people. I was also intrigued by what was then called 'New Journalism,' a style that incorporated fiction narrative techniques."

After a series of internships, Dion landed a job as a night police reporter for the *Hartford Courant* in Connecticut. He worked from 6:00 p.m. to 2:00 a.m., and he loved it. Dion Thompson was a newspaperman. "The paper had a big display window that looked down on the press room. I can remember standing there when I had written a page-one story and rhapsodizing in my mind about how this story would soon be in homes all across Connecticut. Ah, youth!"

Dion spent two and half years at the *Courant*. The high point of his tenure there was not a journalistic achievement. Rather, it was meeting Jean, a fellow journalist who would later become his wife and fellow servant in the Lord's work.

Offered a job at the *Miami Herald*, Dion headed south with Jean, and they were married soon after that. Dion was assigned to cover neighborhoods and crime. It was a good assignment that he thoroughly enjoyed. His reportage even led to the firing of a public housing director. "Whoopee! Of course, someone else replaced this fellow, and the same old stuff continued. What does the Who song say: 'Meet the new boss, same as the old boss.'"

After several years at the *Herald*, Dion was offered a job at the *Baltimore Sun* in Maryland. He was hired to cover the court system. The career thing was going fine.

It was during this time of job transition that another transition began in Dion's life.

"I had been going through a time of spiritual seeking but had not hit upon anything that resonated with my soul. While on vacation in Key West, Florida, I had a holy encounter. It was as if I heard the voice of God saying, 'I hear you've been looking for me. Well, here I am.' Key to my spiritual awakening was my discovery of the *Book of Common Prayer*. I came across it in Key West, opened it, and was amazed to find a prayer for every need. At the time, I had no language for talking to God. The prayer book loosened my tongue."

Back in Baltimore, Dion found himself both unsettled and intrigued by the experience. He visited several Episcopal churches but did not find any "broadcasting on my frequency." A colleague, aware of his search, had written a story about a small church in a converted auto-parts store. She suggested that he attend a service there. So one Sunday, Dion visited the Church of the Holy Nativity.

"Well, my first visit was magical in a frightening way. I knew I had two choices. I could never go back to Holy Nativity, and my life would stay on its course. And I knew that if I went back to the church, something would happen. I didn't know what. But I was sure something would happen. I kept going back. Sunday after Sunday, having not gone to church regularly for twenty-five-plus years, I would find myself at Holy Nativity, listening to a chanted Eucharist, breathing in the incense, and wondering what was happening. Sometimes I felt like I was being pulled by some sort of magnet."

The magnet was a call to the ministry, a call Dion resisted at first. But "curiosity got the better of me." Eventually, curiosity gave way to commitment. So in 2003, Dion Thompson wrote his last newspaper story, posted his last byline, and resigned to prepare for seminary. "I had gone far in journalism. But my spiritual compass was turning in another direction. God saw in me a heart that wanted to help His children. He gave me an opportunity to live in a fuller, more passionate and spiritual way."

Dion spent the next year preparing for the seminary and writing his first novel, *Walk Like a Natural Man*.

In 2007, Dion finished the seminary, graduating with a Master of Divinity degree from The General Theological Seminary. Shortly thereafter, he became the rector at The Church of the Holy Covenant.

Although Dion's newspaper career is now far behind him, he believes God used it in his new career.

"It gave me a chance to mix with all sorts of people and to be comfortable with all sorts of people. In a way, my growing up was also part of this preparation. Being a journalist and writer allowed me to be curious about life, our joys and sorrows. The writing skills came in handy during seminary and in sermon preparation. But, more importantly, I gained a sensitivity to humanity. You also might say God led me to a vocation where I could bring all of my talents to bear. Its riches are such that I will never be bored. My curiosity, interest in history, affinity for language, and scholarly leanings will always find something new to feast on."

For a man who once laughed at the idea that he would be called to the ministry, today Dion revels in being part of a great pastoral lineage.

"The Pastoral Epistles are wonderfully instructive and perceptive. Treatises on the priesthood by Jerome, John Chrysostom, and Gregory tell of problems, pitfalls, and joys that exist as much today as in ancient times. In this way, I feel deeply connected to those who have gone before me. The holy moments of the priesthood are transcendent and profound."

Dion Thompson may have laughed all those years ago. But God just smiled. He knew the joke was on Dion.

12

DAVID STECCA
Let the Deaf See

Founder and CEO,
Deaf Video Communications of America

And we know that in all things God works for the
good of those who love him, who have been called
according to his purpose.

Romans 8:28

One Friday evening, Chicago-area police officer Dave Stecca's radio crackled, "D-delta two seven, you have a family domestic at—." The voice on the other end of the assignment was the dispatcher. But, as Dave would learn later, the call was from God.

Dave grew up in a Christian home where "radio permeated our home like a soft summer breeze. It was always there in the background. Daily I heard sermons preached, Bible verses being taught, music, and of course children's programs. Some fifteen years later, Christian radio continued to be a close friend as I cruised the neighborhoods of a Chicago suburb in my squad car. As a police officer, Christian radio became my anchor. I soaked up Bible studies, sermons, and music for eight hours a day. That foundation equipped me as I faced uncertain situations."

One of those situations was the domestic dispute call on that Friday evening. Dave arrived to find a husband and wife flailing at each other as they made strange noises he had never heard before. Three very young children huddled in a corner. The oldest stepped up and cried, "Please help me. My mom and dad are fighting. My mom and dad are *deaf*."

"Deaf! At the police department, we had interpreters available to us for every spoken language represented in the community, but no interpreters for the deaf. So this little girl became my interpreter." Because neither parent could read or write, the little girl interpreted for her parents all the way through the processing. The situation moved Dave.

"I asked my wife, Ruby, if she would be willing to learn sign language with me. And that began our journey into the 'world' of the deaf. We later found ourselves interpreting in churches, courtrooms, hospitals, teaching a deaf Sunday School class, and conducting a deaf Bible study in our home. I was even called in at the last minute by a young deaf mother to interpret for her in the delivery room. To my relief, Ruby arrived and replaced me in the nick of time. Unknown to me, God had started moving me from a police car to a mission field. The transition took several years and was not simple or comfortable."

The complications began just as Dave and Ruby were preparing for the first real Christmas with their one-year-old daughter, Sherry Jeanette. Ruby was diagnosed with Hodgkin's lymphoma. The prognosis gave her a year, maybe five with treatment. "I spent much of that Christmas, and many Christmases after that, locked in the bathroom crying." After surgeries and extended radiation treatments, the doctors announced that Ruby was in temporary remission. But it was short-lived, and soon Ruby began an aggressive regimen of "MOPP" chemotherapy (a combination chemotherapy composed of mustargen, oncovin, procarbazine, and prednisone).

"During this, in the middle of what was the struggle of our lives, God started tugging at my heart. To do what? Go where? That was unclear. With a sick wife and a four-year-old daughter, my job was the only security and stability I had. All I knew was that God was calling me to leave the work I loved and trust Him. I needed some heavy-duty convincing. So I set out five fleeces. The first fleece was met when an event in my police department caused me to become disenchanted with my job. When God met the remaining four, I realized I had no choice but to obey. I set my resignation date ahead six months to give God one last chance to change His mind."

Shortly before Dave was to leave the force, he was dispatched to handle the complaint of an illegally parked vehicle, a task he accepted reluctantly. As he left the call, he spotted a Winnebago truck parked in a driveway. "What really got my attention was the symbol of the Holy Spirit painted on the side of the truck." Dave went up to the house and was greeted by an unsettled but friendly young man who informed him that the truck was a production van that belonged to a Christian television company. He showed Dave around the truck and gave him the name and phone number of the company's owner. Fascinated, Dave contacted the owner and the next weekend sat in the truck watching a television program being produced.

"Within a few weeks, I had left the police force for good. The only thing I knew how to do, with my background in forensic photography, was take pictures. So I cashed in my pension and hung my shingle on the door as a forensic and commercial photographer. Nine months later, I was broke, had no contracts, and yet another Christmas was on its way. Ruby was fighting stage 3–4 lymphoma, and there wasn't enough cash to buy my daughter a Christmas present. I was at my lowest point in my familiar spot in the bathroom, angry at God. Somehow the television truck came to mind; maybe, just maybe he would remember me and find some place for me to work."

The owner did remember Dave and hired him to help during his busy Christmas season of productions. The job lasted much longer, and eventually Dave, having learned every aspect of video production, became crew chief for the video truck. As his skills grew, so did his reputation. In time, the Chicago Police Department asked David to work for them making training videos on homicide investigation.

"It was my dream come true. It combined my old police skills and my newly discovered video production skills. But something wasn't right. This wasn't what God had in mind, was it? I knew it wasn't. I needed to trust God more, but for what...when...where?"

When the series of videos was completed, Dave turned to still photography, building a solid reputation as a commercial photographer. At the same time, however, Ruby's health was sliding again. Nearly five years of surgeries, maximum amounts of radiation and chemotherapy, and an inability to eat solid foods had left her bedridden. Dave cut back on his work to spend as much time with her as he could. One night as a drained Dave lay sleeping next to Ruby, he sensed that she was not breathing. "I couldn't find a pulse."

On this trip to the hospital, the doctors informed Dave that the chemotherapy had destroyed Ruby's immune system and that she had only a few hours to live.

"God had other plans. Ruby spent the night in a refrigerator bed to bring down her fever, with IVs in every vein that chemo hadn't destroyed. And covered by the prayers of friends and family around the world. Thirty-six hours later, Ruby was conscious. Her fever had broken, she had little baby white cells growing in her system, and the cancer was gone! It took a full year for her to recover, but it was a complete recovery. It was an impossible recovery."

Now, with Ruby fully healed, God was ready for Dave to bring all the experiences and tools he had been given to serve Him. From the "domestic dispute" that led him to learn sign language to the video experience, God was ready for Dave to use all of it.

"I was in my car listening to Christian radio, in particular a Bible study. I listened intently; this was the same passage I planned to use in the deaf Sunday School class I was teaching. As I listened, I began to ask God, 'How can I give to my Sunday School class the lesson I was listening to on the radio?" The radio teacher was far more educated and skilled at teaching than I would ever be. All the deaf class had was me, unskilled, untrained, and barely able to communicate in their language. Gently, God spoke to my heart and asked me, 'What do you know how to do?' Make videos. 'Why not make videos in sign language for the deaf?' That was it. That is what God wanted me to do."

In 1983, with Ruby by his side, Dave founded Deaf Video Communications of America, Inc., a not-for-profit mission agency dedicated to proclaiming the Gospel to the deaf visually in their own language—sign language.

"Equipped with a home VHS recorder and camera, we began videotaping pastors, evangelists, and teachers as they preached and taught God's Word. We added American Sign Language. Very quickly the word began to spread throughout the deaf community that we had VHS tapes in ASL for the deaf. Requests for tapes came in from all fifty states and many countries. The DVC Lending Library was established as a free lending library to handle the now nearly sixty thousand requests we received for videos."

Today, DVC has its own building near Wheaton, Illinois. The DVC Deaf Ministry Center houses the DVC Lending Library, a professional video-production studio and tech department, as well as a conference center complete with a dormitory, conference rooms, and kitchens.

And Dave's affection for the radio, where he first learned about the Lord, has become another part of the DVC ministry with www.dvc.tv, a Christian "radio" station for the deaf. Children's programs, Bible studies, marriage and family videos, devotions, and sermons are proclaiming the Gospel visually in sign language to the deaf around the world twenty-four/seven.

"Our walk by faith has taken us through some very deep valleys. For us it seemed that our deepest valleys occurred right after a test and decisive choice to follow God wherever He leads. After each test, each valley, God was there to turn our experience into something beautiful and wonderful."

And into a rare blessing for the deaf, who can now enjoy videos about their faith and the Lord they love…all thanks to a cop who responded to a call.

13

NANCY KREBS
God's Troubadour
Christian Music Composer and Performer

And Mary said, "My soul magnifies the Lord, and my spirit has rejoiced in God my Savior."

Luke 1:46–48

Actors feed off their egos. They have to if they are to succeed. And actress Nancy Krebs was no exception. That was God's hook. "God knew He could entice me through my ego. He's smart that way." He did entice Nancy. Right into His service.

The oldest of seven children, Nancy grew up in an encouraging home. "Our parents were extremely supportive of all our interests and must have driven themselves crazy just trying to keep up with seven very active kids. It must have been a mad house, looking back on it, but lots of fun."

Nancy's interests were broad: reading adventure novels, exploring with telescopes and microscopes, learning the violin and guitar, and theater. "I loved softball, too, although my dad wouldn't let me play the catcher position, which I really enjoyed, because he didn't want me to injure my hands. I guess he was thinking about a future career for me as a violinist." At thirteen, Nancy's interest in theater began to trump some of her other interests, and her acting career began to bud.

Born a "cradle Catholic" and surrounded by relatives who took their faith seriously, religion was a part of the fabric in her life from a very early age. "God was a constant in my life." And so was her church. In her teen years, Nancy became a member of the first phalanx of the Folk Mass musicians who brought guitar into services for the first time. And she began to compose songs with spiritual themes.

"Contemplating and reflecting when composing a song brought me closer to the realization that God was more present in my life, not just for favors or to answer prayers, but as an entity of love. He became more real and more personal. Even though most of the songs from those early years have not survived the test of time, due mainly to the fact that I was depending on my own powers of inspiration, that period of time gave me an opportunity to really think about the Lord and to develop an awareness of His presence in my everyday life as a guiding force. And that relationship began to take on more meaning for me in those formative years."

When Nancy finished high school, she left for college to study acting and singing. She continued her acting studies into graduate school. Not satisfied with just knowing how to act, Nancy wanted her voice and body to be refined tools that would give her an even greater edge as a performer, so she continued studying even while performing, becoming a Master Teacher in Lessac Kinesensic Training.

"I truly loved using my imagination and my physical and vocal skills to create three-dimensional characters that would have an impact on audiences. I especially loved plays that shared a strong positive message and always felt that I was part of a team of artists who shared the common goal of service. I felt that we were a breed apart, specially designated as purveyors of insight into the ecstasies, foibles, and faults of the human condition. To me, theater is a noble profession."

Nancy's career was successful by most all actors' standards. It's a tough arena and, over time, unable to turn it into a living, most people drop out.

"I was always very fortunate to be a 'working actor' during my theatrical career. I was never without a job. I worked in dinner theater, regional theater, TV, and did a little movie work, a lot of voice-over work, and educational theater."

Completely focused on her acting and singing career, Nancy let the spiritual side of her musical life slide away. "I thought I had left my 'church-singing' days behind me when I graduated from the university, ready to launch my theater career. How wrong I was!" Still tied to the basic concepts of faith from her childhood, she did what many people in their twenties and thirties do: she church-hopped. She eventually landed back at her birth parish, where she was asked to consider providing meditational music during the services. She was flattered to be asked. God had set the bait.

"A funny thing happened. I began to fall in love with the liturgies and the Blessed Trinity by beginning once again to write songs with spiritual themes. As I mentioned, as a teenager I had written songs for services, but I had relied on my own 'powers of inspiration,' which were pretty insignificant. But this time, I asked God: 'Father, Son, Holy Spirit—what do you want me to write?' And this wellspring of inspiration began to flow. I started reading books and articles written by spiritually minded authors, listened more intently to the sermons delivered by gifted preachers, and read more deeply the Old and New Testaments. All this gave a depth to the songwriting that didn't exist before. I turned the process of writing over to God, and He didn't disappoint."

Still committed to her theatrical career and, unlike many actors, staying busy with regular bookings, Nancy's stage work still commanded most of her attention. And it paid the bills. But something was changing for her, and she knew it.

"When I began writing spiritually driven songs once again, theater projects felt less important. Even the subjects for most plays didn't thrill me as they once did. I was thrown into a kind of midlife crisis. If acting wasn't satisfying me anymore, what would be satisfying? What did God want me to do with the rest of my life? These questions haunted me more and more. Finally, it became clearer that music ministry was the road I was intended to travel. My first love had been music, so it was as if I was coming full circle, back to what I initially had been doing—making music."

In 1998, Nancy and her husband, Pete, produced her first CD, *The Journey*. She began to take concert dates and embarked on a "spiritual journey in song.'" Since then, she has released seven other CDs, held hundreds of concerts, and represented the United States in the World Festival of Marian Songs. She has also traveled to Italy as minister of music for spiritual pilgrimages.

"Looking back over the many years of my acting career, it looks like a quilt to me now. The pieces are all there that led to this 'career' in my music ministry. All the different skills that I learned along the way have made an appearance once again in music ministry. I have a feeling I was meant to do this all along, but I just ignored the signs and the many suggestions from our Lord. I know He was trying to guide me in this direction when I was a teenager, but I deliberately turned another way. Often I wish that I hadn't ignored that small voice. But if I hadn't had the performance career I did, I might not be as prepared or as mature spiritually to do what I'm doing now. God really took me on a ride, but it was a good ride, and filled with excitement and joy."

Today, Nancy's music and songs are played on the radio throughout the world. And she continues to look for, and discover, new venues in which to serve and share the music of God. And what about that ego God used to serve for His call to Nancy?

"Now I want to be invisible as I sing. I simply want to be what the twelfth-century mystic, writer, and liturgical composer Hildegard von Bingen describes as a 'feather on the breath of God.' I'll try to do what He wants me to do, secure in the knowledge that He knows best what my journey should be."

Nancy Krebs, troubadour for the Lord.

14

WARREN MUELLER
Touched by the Untouchable
Anglican Priest

I am the way, the truth, and the life. No one comes to the Father but through me.

John 14:6

How did a man who had pursued a doctorate in chemical physics and a career in research and marketing wind up ministering to people with special needs? Through a remarkable journey with an unusual start.

"Although I had come to Christ in a very profound conversion experience in 1988, my subsequent journey in Christ had been very self-absorbed as a biblically, theologically, and liturgically literate Christian. That would change, in a sneaky sort of way. One Sunday, the women in my home parish in Baton Rouge asked folks to get involved in a new HIV/AIDS ministry group. I ignored their pleas because of my own aversion to dealing with sick folks."

Not long after that, they mentioned that a client they were working with needed his lawn mower repaired and didn't have the money to buy a new one. Because Warren was a "fix-it sort of guy," he approached them and said he could do that. So one of the ministry-group members delivered the mower to Warren's house, and he was able to repair the engine.

"I took the mower back to the client's house, as no one else was available to do that. There, I met the client; a guy in his early thirties who was quite frail, weak, and sick. While chatting with him, being careful not to touch anything, I learned that he had some other things around his house that needed fixing. I helped with those items. Slowly, step by step, God was drawing me into service ministry."

In 1980, Warren got married in a civil ceremony to a woman with two daughters by a previous marriage. The marriage started well. They bought a house and established what seemed to be a typical suburban life.

"By 1985, we were having difficulty with our marriage, and I was doing a considerable amount of work-related travel, with much of it being extended trips overseas. In 1987, my wife moved out of the house, and we were divorced in 1989."

The separation and process toward divorce was crushing for Warren to accept. His parents had a wonderful marriage of more than fifty years and were totally devoted to each other. As the weeks and months of endless legal fighting continued, Warren began to seriously question what possibly could be the purpose of the incredible suffering he was enduring. "What was the point of life, if this is all there is?"

At this point, two important things happened. First, Warren's parents and his younger brother, Roger, moved from St. Petersburg, Florida, to Orlando. Second, Roger became deeply involved in the Episcopal Cathedral of St. Luke in Orlando. He ran the Cathedral Book Store and was the administrator for the Diocesan School of Ministry. Roger's mom was doing her usual volunteer work there.

"During a visit with Roger, I was overwhelmed with how happy he was about life. He was dirt poor, but he just radiated a happiness and joy for life that seemed intimately connected to his church life. I began to examine my life in contrast to my brother's. Although I had never ceased to believe in God, I began to realize that I had certainly shut myself off from God in my life. I had apparently come to believe, partly as a function of my intensive scientific training, that I could run my affairs just fine without God's help. And certainly, until my marriage fell apart, that illusion had served me quite well.

"With this small personal epiphany, the influence of my parents' devotion to faithful church worship kicked in, and at my lowest ebb ever in my life, I literally picked an Episcopal church out of the phone book to attend. I even prayed a little for God's help to show me how I needed to amend my life—if He would help me."

God had to have been with Warren on that first Sunday when he walked into St. Luke's Episcopal Church in Baton Rouge, Louisiana, to attend the 8:00 a.m. service.

"Miracles sure did happen for me that day. I had no idea how, but somehow I knew I was going to be all right. Not only had I accepted Christ into my life, not only had my life been saved by Christ, but I realized it was actually possible to feel the actual presence of God all around me."

Indeed, the presence of God was so strong that Warren, after serving there as a lay minister for a number of years, decided to proceed with the process for ordination to the diaconate. He was ordained in 1999 and was allowed to continue serving at St. Luke's. Because the deacon's position did not include a salary, he also continued working at his commercial job. However, within two years, he was laid off.

About this same time, his father, still living in Orlando, became increasingly ill. Warren realized he needed to be with his father and mother during that time and transferred his canonical residency to the Diocese of Central Florida.

"That change, that move, that huge, sudden discontinuity, was absolutely essential for placing me on the path I am on today. Had I stayed in Baton Rouge, serving where I was serving, I would probably still be there serving in that same role. Not that that would be bad, but it would be just what it was. Apparently that was not to be the case, thanks be to God.

"In 2007, my mother, living by herself in Orlando after my dad died in 2004, called me up one day and announced that she wanted to come live near my wife, Nan, and me. So we found her a little place to live a few minutes from our house and had her moved in by mid-2007."

In 2009, Warren's mother was diagnosed with early dementia and a form of Parkinson's. By mid-2010, she needed 24/7 care. Instead of putting her in a nursing home, which she detested, Warren and Nan became her caregivers. "It was very difficult and exhausting. As difficult as the process of caring for her was for Nan and me, through that process came the inspiration, or call, for planting Resurrection Anglican Church on the Gulf and the mission of that church."

That path has led Warren into a unique mission beyond the church's established mission statement, "bringing all to Christ."

"Part of that mission is to create a welcoming and accommodating place for those who live with functional disabilities, their family members, and/or their caregivers. In addition to being welcoming and accommodating, we also want to be empowering. That is, we want to create an environment where everyone can respond to God's call in their lives, despite the functional disabilities that are trying to hold them back. For example, if a visually impaired person wanted to read the scripture lessons, we would find a way to use technology for them to do so. If someone in a wheelchair wanted to serve as a lay Eucharistic minister, we would work with them to enable that call in their life. The core action coming out of our mission is to let those who have withdrawn from church life come back to the church. They often withdraw because the hassles of going to church because surmounting barriers to the disabled are too great. Also, they just may feel very out of place and feel that they aren't welcome."

Not at Fr. Warren Mueller's church. The engineer who was afraid to be with the ill and infirm is now God's messenger of His love for them.

15

LISA ROBERTS
Lobbyist for Christ
Founding Partner, Church Partners Foundation

*Put on a heart of compassion, kindness, humility,
gentleness, and patience; bearing with one another,
and forgiving each other, whoever has a complaint
against anyone; just as the Lord forgave you, so also
should you. Beyond all these things put on love,
which is the perfect bond of unity.*

Colossians 3:12–14

"On December 27, 2007, alone in my Crystal City apartment, I hit a wall. A wall so tall and so strong that I knew there was no going through, over, or around it. It was squarely in my face. I was done. I remember being angry. I was really at the top of my game professionally, I thought. I had a great job, making good money. I loved my boss, my office, my colleagues. And we were going places. Crying, I fell to my knees."

On that cold winter night, Lisa Roberts, despite all of her worldly success, knew what had been missing from her life. Although she had been brought up in a home with an agnostic mother and an atheist father, Lisa had been a Christian since high school.

"My faith journey began with a friend's invitation when I was in high school. Admittedly, because my parents were very strict and wouldn't allow me to go out much, I used the opportunity to attend worship at a local church and a Young Life club just to get away from my parents. As I became immersed in these communities, however, I developed friendships that last to this day, and a relationship with Christ. I formally accepted Jesus as my Savior and was baptized when I was sixteen."

After high school, Lisa pursued a degree in English. God continued to be a presence in her life, but only a slight presence. She was young and invincible. "I took God on a pretty wild ride. My life has been a pretty long and winding road…some on the path He lit for me, and some not so much."

College completed, Lisa took a job in corporate management with Nabisco. While working there, she volunteered at local nonprofits, often working alongside her grandmother. "She helped me appreciate the value of giving time and money to those who are less fortunate." During her seventh year with Nabisco, Lisa was part of a major employee layoff. While she looked for another job, she volunteered at Junior Achievement, eventually accepting their job offer to become development director.

"Little did I know that that decision would direct me to a career path that was both meaningful and rewarding. I loved being able to see tangible evidence that my life mattered and that I could make a difference by helping individuals who were less fortunate than me. My career in nonprofit was, and is, an extension of who I am."

Over the next two decades, Lisa immersed herself in the nonprofit world of children's advocacy. Her work managing organizations that provided educational programs for at-risk and disadvantaged youth led to the development of two national model programs. She was a presenter at national and international educational advocacy and career-development programs. So well regarded was her work that she was offered, and accepted, a full fellowship to pursue an MBA. Upon graduation, Lisa was recruited to join a national think tank in Columbus, Ohio.

In a little more than a year, she was recruited again, this time by a national think tank that dealt with state-level policy in each state. They wanted her to set up a similar organization in, and specifically for, Montana. Within a year, the Montana Policy Institute was incorporated and thriving. Lisa was making things happen, and it was being noticed where the big-time policy decisions were being made every day.

In 2006, Lisa moved to Washington, DC. There she joined the highly regarded Tax Foundation as development director. Now she was a player in the most powerful city in the world. She attended meetings with high-profile decision makers, cocktail parties at the right clubs, and dinners with notables at five-star restaurants. And she lived in an apartment that faced just across the river to the lights of the "shining city on a hill." Yet on that cold December night, Lisa Roberts was lonely and knew something was missing. And she fell to her knees.

"And I prayed. I expressed every bit of loneliness, despair, and anger to God in a way I never had. And I fully surrendered. Not in the 'raise your finger if you're a sinner' Baptist kind of surrender, but a real surrender. I knew that I wasn't supposed to be in DC, but I didn't know where God wanted me to be, so I offered my life, my desires, my everything to Him in that moment.

"The next few days are a fog. My birthday passed, and the New Year rang in, but I can't recall details, except for one. I received a call on January third from a friend in my hometown of Jacksonville, Florida. He serves on a board for a nonprofit there. They were looking for a VP. Was I interested? Wow! Really? I never let myself be homesick, but I think I frequently was, and now I could go back. Two days later, I received two more calls from colleagues with leads for jobs in Florida. All unsolicited. How did they know? I accepted the job in Jacksonville and left DC in March 2008, convinced that God wanted me in Florida."

Once there, God's plan for Lisa began to unfold. "It was like a domino effect." Professionally, Lisa was happy to be where she was. Spiritually, she was comfortable that she was following God's plan, whatever that was. Personally, she was fine, too. After several relationships had gone sour in Washington, she was content that maybe she was supposed to focus on her professional career for a while. Little did she know that God was just beginning her journey.

"During that week of contemplation and surrender in 2007, I checked several old e-mail addresses, and one of them was classmates.com. I had some messages from a few old friends, including a high school friend named Tim. He was congenial and sweet and, in his closing, he reminded me of our special history. It was at my persuasion that Tim had chosen to attend a Young Life meeting with me during high school—a decision that he, to this day, credits as the first step toward his first step toward answering a call to ministry and a life of faith that we both cherish. I responded with a brief update on my life, as well as expressing surprise that he was a pastor, and promised to stay in touch. Little did I know that that e-mail would be the catalyst to a future that only God could design. A future with such intricate details that only He could weave. In retrospect, it is both amazing and humbling."

Once she was back in Florida, Lisa and Tim met for lunch. "My mind was reeling at that point. It's 2008, we're having lunch. We're reconnecting. I'm talking about my desire to converge my spiritual gifts with my professional experience and pursue the life God has planned for me. For the next six or so months, we continued to have lunch, chat, pray…and then it became very clear. We were being called together for something. We prayed. And waited. And, sure enough, God, being the awesome God that He is, continued to open doors and light our path."

Shortly after relocating back to Florida, Lisa had

joined a church and quickly assumed a leadership position. As a result of that, she was asked to participate in a statewide clergy-coaching program. She got to know clergy leadership across the state. "Throughout all of this, I knew God was in control and was literally pushing me."

But Lisa wasn't quite ready to move. She had begun a consulting business, and it was becoming very successful. "Still, I knew that God was calling me for something bigger, so I continued to pray. But secretly I thought, 'Gee, this is good! Really, I'm okay with this.'"

Then, in the summer of 2009, God challenged both Lisa and Tim with a call that would engage the experiences, knowledge, and faith each had harvested during their years working in their individual fields. "It became clear to Tim and me that God was calling us to minister to under-resourced churches and new clergy." So in June 2009, they founded the Church Partners Foundation to serve under-resourced churches and mentor young clergy.

The confirmation that they were where God wanted them came quickly. The IRS approval for nonprofit status, which normally can take a year, was granted in forty-five days. And while they were waiting for that decision, the United Methodist Conference of Florida asked them to partner in supporting under-resourced churches in Florida, with all expenses covered. Then, in July 2010, the foundation received a major grant to work with fifty-two churches. God was at work.

"'God is good. All the time. All the time. God is good.' Those words kept ringing in my head. I just couldn't believe the doors that opened. But then again, I knew that all things are possible with God, and I needed to start believing. So I did. And, though the path is clearer than it was two years ago, I'm always a little nervous about the next step. God is stretching me to what feels like my breaking point, but in every case He gives me the strength to move on and reminds me that the discontent in my heart is what steers me."

God had a plan for Lisa on that cold December night. He knew that His plan for Lisa, and for Tim, would not only make them partners in His work, but married partners in life too.

When Lisa chose to follow His plan, the "wall came a-tumblin' down."

16

FRED RAMSAY
A Twist Here, A Turn There
Retired Episcopal Priest, Mystery Writer

Show me your ways, O Lord, teach me your paths:
Guide me in your truth and teach me.

Psalm 25:4–5

Fred Ramsay's call to Christian ministry has the earmarks of one of his mystery books—twists and turns that seem misdirecting, yet string together to build the story. They share an underlying thread of continuity that, in the end, help answer many questions and lead to a satisfying conclusion.

The story begins on a private school campus in the rolling countryside just northwest of Baltimore, Maryland. It was an idyllic setting with both advantages and disadvantages for the Ramsay boy. Fred recalls the advantages outweighing the latter, just the way every child should remember his or her growing-up years.

Like most of the other children in his day and in his circumstances, young Fred was a church-goer. "Only the very odd or suspiciously eccentric did not attend church with their mothers. Dads were mostly Christmas and Easter Christians unless, of course, they were Catholics. For reasons that were not then, and are not to this very day, clear, I was an acolyte for some of those years."

In an incident of foreshadowing worthy of a fine

mystery, the parish priest predicted that young Ramsay would enter the ranks of the clergy. "It was a prediction my mother met with consternation and my father with laughter."

Fred attended Washington and Lee University, majoring in biology. As with most students, his college years were tailored to his scholastic and social interests. It was a full agenda that left him with no time, or inclination, to pursue any particular interest in religion. He did continue going to church, but irregularly and mostly as a matter of habit. Neither the church's effort to reach out to its attendees nor the priest's sermons impressed him much.

After completing college, Fred enrolled in the graduate program at the University of Illinois. He earned a master's degree and a PhD in anatomy, then another master's degree in education. He was on track to a career in research and teaching. The clues to Fred's immediate career were becoming clear. Coming equally clear, if not so methodically honed, was another aspect of Fred's life, one that would have an even greater bearing on his future: his relationship with God.

"My journey to a heightened understanding of God closely resembled a very slow swallowing up by spiritual quicksand. Something—an event, a dropped phrase, a set of circumstances in someone else's life—caused me step forward, and then another one and another, and finally it had me."

After a stint in the US Army, Fred began the career he had prepared for. He took a job at the University of Maryland School of Medicine. He taught anatomy, embryology, and histology. He also worked as a researcher. In time, Fred moved to the dean's office, where he served in several roles, including Director of Medical Education, Associate Dean of Student Affairs and, finally, Associate Dean for Governmental Liaison.

Fred was having the kind of successful career that would fulfill most people. But there was another aspect to his life that was increasingly causing him to question where he was with all of this. The quicksand that had swallowed him up for the Lord was now moving him toward a call to serve well beyond being an example. And, though he didn't quite understand why that was, he accepted that he had to move with it.

"As with most of the things I have tackled in my lifetime, I never gave it a thought. I am one who sails with the wind. God wants me here? Here I am. Perhaps not particularly well prepared. Perhaps not well planned. But so be it."

Without a clear sense of what he was to do with this call, Fred did feel that the priesthood was where he needed to be. So he met with his former parish priest—the same one who had predicted years earlier that a young Ramsay would one day become a priest.

The snag in moving forward was that Fred was in no position to leave his job and attend seminary. A meeting with the local bishop led to a solution. It appeared that five other career men, also in Fred's position, shared his interest in studying for the priesthood. So they set up a night-school seminary for this group of "over-thirty" seminarians. Fred continued his job at the university by day and began his studies for priesthood at night.

During this time of simultaneously building his career at the medical school and studying for the priesthood, Fred felt strongly that he had been put in this dual role to stand for Christ. "By that I mean there was no doubt that I represented a spiritual position or belief set and was available and/or willing to defend and proclaim it, if asked. The sad fact of the matter, however, was that I was rarely asked to do so. Perhaps just being there was enough. I'll never know. But God is sure, even if we aren't, and He moved me along."

In 1969, Fred finished "reading for orders" and was subsequently ordained an Episcopal priest. He left the university and a successful twenty-five-year career in medical education. "I felt like I was meeting myself coming around the corner, and it was time to go and see what God had in store for me. After that, I spent the remainder of my career years in a traditional church setting. I thoroughly enjoyed it. It gave me opportunities to both teach and preach."

Fr. Ramsay is one of the six authors of *The Baltimore Declaration*, a "95 thesis"-type affirmation of orthodox Christianity. Delivered by this select group of priests who felt the Episcopal Church had abandoned the Christian faith, it still stands as a bold and challenging document. "I earned the Bishop's Award, in spite of it, and eventually retired content."

Today, Fred looks back on his earlier career in medical education not so much as some twist in the plot of his story to God's service but as another example of the "proof that spirituality can, and does, coexist with practicality, within the same universe of ideas, even within the same person." He sums it up in a lecture titled "Merging the Spiritual and the Empirical: Thinking Paradoxically in a Binary World." "It's not widely attended, but it makes the point."

Fred reflects on his call to Christian ministry with the mind of a scientist and the heart of a pastor. "If you believe, as I do, that God uses you as He sees fit, any attempt to establish cause and effect between what you're about and what you think needs doing is, and will be, frustrating. Judging from the way God lassoed me, it is my belief that He is a lot smarter than we are and a lot more forgiving than we are, and in the end, He will overlook ignorance or stupidity on our part if it is driven, however mistakenly, by compassion."

Like any good mystery writer, Fred has a capacity for tying up all the loose ends into a succinct, revealing moment, whether for one of his stories or to understand God's call: "To know Him is to submit. To submit is to never question."

17

SUSAN RAMSAY
"Not Yet," He Said
Episcopal Diaconate

I rejoiced when they said to me, "Let us go to the house of the Lord."

Psalm 122:1

Susan Ramsay is witness to the phenomenon of God calling just when you think it's time to put your feet up and relax. After decades of following the Lord's will for her life, Susan and her pastor husband retired and settled in a warm climate, nestled in for reaping the rewards of a lifetime spent in His service. What she didn't know was that the Lord still had more sowing for her to do.

Susan grew up in a churched environment. Her grandparents were both contributors to her Christian foundation during her childhood years. It was they who saw to it that she and her six siblings made it to Sunday School each week. Like many teenagers in those times, Susan was confirmed in her teen years, graduated from high school, and went off to college to prepare for a career and graduate into the rest of life. Unlike many teenagers, Susan lost her mother while still a sophomore in college. In spite the difficulty of such an untimely loss, she continued with her education, finishing with a degree in elementary education. "I chose elementary education because I could explore a variety of interests, albeit with children. Having summers off was also an attractive aspect."

Her post-college life followed the form of the era. She taught, met and married her husband, had children, and gave up her career to be a vocational mom.

In what was an otherwise fulfilling life, there remained one troubling area. And, it seemed, it shouldn't have been. Susan had grown up spiritually nurtured. Her husband, Fred, was an Episcopal priest, and she was a supportive minister's wife. All of this, yet there was still an unresolved issue in Susan's faith life. "Although I had attended church all my life, still, I had my doubts."

Susan did what many others do with unsettled heavenly questions. She put them aside to address the more earthly, day-to-day matters.

One of those matters was returning to the workforce. Initially, she stayed within her comfort zone, working in the education field—in college admissions, alumni affairs, and fund-raising.

In time, however, she was lured out of education and into an alien discipline: business aviation. It was a unique opportunity, and Susan took the job. Her new career gave her opportunities to expand her knowledge and experience in customer service, marketing, and training. It was interesting and energizing work, and she took advantage of the chance to both grow in her job and contribute to the business. "The highlight of that career was to serve as chair of a standing committee at the annual conference for the National Business Aviation Association." The career change worked out well for Susan, professionally and personally. And it gave her tools she would need in a career she had no idea was coming.

At just about the same time as she began her business aviation job, she experienced another transforming event in her life. Along with some other Christian friends, Susan attended a Cursillo weekend. "It was there that I became convinced that God loved me, and I found myself seeking hard after God." She left the event determined to read the entire Bible to get a sweep of the story, once and for all.

She completed her goal in less than four months. And during those studies, she found resolution for the unresolved issue that had hung over her for so long.

"Reading Isaiah 53, I suddenly realized that Jesus was really who He said He was. Once and for all, the nagging doubts were gone. I felt so ashamed, I knelt down to pray and confessed for two solid hours. When I had finished, it felt as though I had taken the most refreshing shower, that I was cleaner than I'd ever been. It transformed my life."

Susan was indeed transformed. But not yet called. God had more for her to do and learn where she was. Still to come were opportunities to speak in front of large audiences, develop and facilitate training, lead teams, help resolve conflict, and use other tools that ministers use every day in their work, even if they're called by other names in faith circles. God was definitely using this work experience for witnessing and on-the-job training.

"More often than not, it seemed, God was in the mix, giving me an eye for seeing the best in people and a desire to make things better. Frequently, I sensed that God positioned me to express gratitude, encourage, and even pray with and for coworkers and colleagues."

During those years, Susan sometimes sensed a call to the ministry. But she was busy with a demanding career. Plus, she already was in a ministry of sorts. "Being married to an Episcopal priest provided numerous opportunities to participate in women's retreats, lead sessions on prayer, and assist with church services." So she labored on where God had placed her.

After a twenty-year aviation business career, Susan retired. Around the same time, Fred also retired from the ministry. They could relax now and spend more time with each other and the family. Or so they thought.

Shortly after Susan retired, she was asked several times if she had ever considered attending seminary and entering the ministry. The questions were flattering but seemed irrelevant considering her age and where she and Fred were in their lives. "Then one day, my husband received a conference brochure from Trinity School for Ministry titled 'Discerning a Call.' He lay it on my desk without saying anything."

Susan glanced at the brochure, saw that the conference fell the week before they were expecting a family visit, and tossed the brochure in the trash can. "Later, my husband asked me about the brochure, and he spoke to me in a very deliberate tone: 'I think you need to look at it.'"

Later, she retrieved the brochure and read it. "Before I had finished reading it, my heart was drenched. I knew that God was speaking to me. That was the beginning of the discernment process—reading, praying, writing, praying, meeting with others, praying, and finally, being led to Fuller Theological Seminary Southwest in Phoenix."

Susan's calling into vocational Christian service at such a late stage in life seemed a bit peculiar at first. But she knew that a mature woman can have a profound spiritual influence on others. She knew all about that. Her grandmother had taught her well.

"Growing up, I would often spend Sunday afternoons at my grandparents'. My grandmother would watch Billy Graham with an open Bible in her lap. She demonstrated a quiet and steadfast faith that many years later I would try to emulate."

Susan completed her Master of Divinity degree just shy of her sixty-fifth birthday. It turns out that when God said to Susan, "Time to put your feet up," he meant one at a time on a walk to His vocational service.

18

PATRICK CUNNINGHAM
God's Johnny Appleseed
Church Planter

Moses said to the Lord, "O Lord, I have never been eloquent, neither in the past nor since you have spoken to your servant. I am slow of speech and tongue." The Lord said to him, "Who gave man his mouth? Who makes him deaf or mute? Who gives him sight or makes him blind? Is it not I, the Lord? Now go; I will help you speak and will teach you what to say."

Exodus 4:10–12

"You see, for most of my life, I have not only been an introvert but an extremely shy one. I used to say, with absolute honesty, that the ideal job for me would be a lighthouse keeper."

For a young, shy Patrick Cunningham, lighthouse keeper was not as remote a career as it might have seemed.

"I was raised in the Episcopal Church and went to Sunday School until I was confirmed, and then we promptly left the church. After high school, I left for college in the fall and quickly fell into a life of hedonism. My beliefs in college ranged from New Age spiritualism to a form of deism."

After college, Patrick jumped from job to job, career to career, looking for that perfect occupation. Finally, he thought he had settled into a steady, but still unsettling, working life.

"I worked over that time as a laborer, first unskilled then semiskilled. Then as an engineer's assistant, a concrete quality-control tech, assistant to the superintendent of a prestressed concrete plant, manager of the same plant, and then field office manager on various large projects in the Mid-Atlantic."

However, even climbing the corporate ladder didn't seem enough to satisfy his desire for something fulfilling. He moved again, this time establishing a successful career as a risk manager for a large temporary-labor company.

During those hopscotch years, one thing did happen that would be rewarding and that would last. Patrick met and married his sweetheart, Michelle. And that event would change his life even more than he had imagined a marriage might.

"We got married at St. John's, the Episcopal Church that my family had long ties to. We liked the rector, Father Philip Roulette, and his teaching began to bring me back to a basic understanding of the Gospel. So, under twenty years of his tutelage, I became, at least, God-positive."

Becoming God-positive was not the only change in Patrick's church life at St. John's. As Fr. Roulette's Gospel-centered ministry drew closer to retirement, a vocal number of members caused inner theological turmoil. A battle arose between those who had a Gospel-centered view of the church and those who wished to deviate from historical teachings. This created a fault line in the congregation. And it was the moment that changed Patrick's life.

"I was serving as a member of the church's vestry. It was a position I was totally unprepared and unqualified for. There I was, a confirmed introvert and a lukewarm Christian, asked to serve on the governing board of the church. I used to sit in those meetings in a state of barely controlled horror. I was really unsettled by what I thought was a stable and healthy church body beginning to turn on itself in a most un-Christian manner. I was terrified to say anything, and equally as terrified to say nothing. I was intimidated by most of the rest of the vestry and petrified by what the others were thinking of me. I got to a point where I began to pray the same prayer driving to those awful meetings: 'Please, Lord, give me the power to say something tonight!' But each night, my mind would freeze, and my mouth would remain silent. I would try to stand, and there would be no strength in my legs."

In time, Fr. Roulette retired and was followed by an interim priest, Fr. 'Chip' Nix. Soon after he arrived at St. John's, Chip organized a men's canoe/camping trip. Patrick hated camping but felt he had to go. "I had a very persistent feeling that I now understand was the Holy Spirit working, telling me that I needed to get to know Chip." Patrick's friendship with Chip did grow closer. And so did his relationship with the Lord.

"For the first time in my life, the Gospel came alive, and a fire was lit in my life for Jesus!"

Patrick enjoyed Chip's Bible-based ministry, but he still sensed a restlessness in the congregation…a sense that the people who pushed for Fr. Roulette's retirement were no happier with Chip. Worse, at the same time, the Episcopal Church was moving away from its own founding doctrines. A small group began praying together for God's guidance about whether they could stay in the church and still remain faithful to their beliefs. Soon, "it became clear to several of us that we were being called to leave the church and plant a new one." Patrick found himself in a position he never thought would be his.

"I will never forget the night that I was called to serve. We were having a general discussion about the pros and cons of what we were considering. I, of course, was sitting in the back of the room. A dear friend of mine had just stood up and given a very logical and reasonable argument about why we should not do it. After he finished speaking, I found myself standing up. My mouth opened, and the words began to flow. For the first time in my life, I was speaking with authority, power, and eloquence that was not my own. The Lord used me as an instrument to not only refute my friend's statements but to make it clear to all in the room that the only way forward was to follow Christ and plant His new church."

Patrick had moved from the shy boy to the man in charge. He led, people followed, and a new church was planted. The group that came with him was very talented and filled with a variety of gifts and accomplishments. It included people who had been wardens or the heads of various important ministries. "By any kind of worldly standard, I should have been the last person anyone would have chosen to be our leader."

But he was. And God had an even greater plan for the reluctant servant. During the years of planting and helping grow Church of the Resurrection in Timonium, Maryland, Patrick sought the council of Fr. Tom Herrick, the founder of an organization called the Titus Institute for Church Planting. Tom needed help with his growing organization. And he sought out Patrick.

Today, Patrick is Regional Director for the Institute's planting work in Maryland, Delaware, and southeastern Pennsylvania. "I coach church leaders who are either planting churches or are having issues within their established churches."

There's an old hymn with these words: "Let the lower lights be burning. Send a gleam across the waves. Some poor struggling, suffering seaman, you may rescue, you may save."

So it turns out that the introverted boy who thought he would best be a lighthouse keeper *is* one.

19

NITA DEMPSEY
Just As I Was

Office Manager,
Society of Anglican Missionaries and Senders (SAMS)

Yet the Lord longs to be gracious to you; therefore he
will rise up to show you compassion. For the Lord is
a God of justice. Blessed are all who wait for him!
Isaiah 30:18

The Easter appeal letter opened this way: "I had a radical conversion. Twice. I know we only get saved once and for all, but it felt like another conversion when I rededicated my life to Christ twenty-four years ago. I was young when I first came to a saving knowledge of Jesus. It was during the Jesus movement of the seventies, and I went to a church that met in the basement of a building filled with converted hippies. It was cool. It felt great to know that I had eternal salvation and also that I had a purpose. However, after a year and a half, I began to fall away. I had succumbed to peer pressure and began my odyssey through the valley of the shadow of death." The letter was from the Society of Anglican Missionaries and Senders. It was signed "Nita Dempsey, Office Manager."

Nita, it turned out, had much more to tell about her faith journey.

"My odyssey started with a broken heart. My family was dysfunctional. I grew up with both parents becoming alcoholics. My parents had become emotionally distant as a result of their drinking. They loved me and were not out making fools of themselves. On one side, I had great experiences that many kids never had. I had culture and music, intellect and art, and religion as a part of my life, all through my parents. Most of all, I had their love. And eventually, because of my mother's prayers, I came to the Lord. In the end, all six of us siblings are born-again Christians. On the other hand, I had terrible experiences that other kids never had. As a young teen, I was not able to talk to either parent about my hurts or my questions. I wanted to know that I was special, so I sought out others who could affirm who I was."

One of those "others" was the Lord. Nita was afraid, and she felt she could find what she needed with Him. But the relationship was short. Nita didn't "grow enough in my faith to know that He was all I needed." So she began looking elsewhere for a connection with something that would make her feel secure. At first, she turned to boys. One of those high school sweethearts with whom she became emotionally attached ended up being obsessive and, eventually, abusive.

"At this same time, our group of friends was experimenting with drugs, and I thought, 'What fun!' and went along with the crowd. No one could have told me at the time that I was trying to escape or run from anything, but I was. I was doing quite a few different drugs, from marijuana to mescaline."

Her relationship with the boy ended, but her drug use did not. It decreased. But drinking filled the drug vacuum. Then she met and began dating the man who would become her first husband. Things seemed to calm. But then the drug use began again, and eventually they escalated it. And the drug of choice changed.

"This time, we were hooked on cocaine. For me, this lifestyle did not last as long as it did for my husband because I was seeing that people we began to hang out with to get the drug, and do it, were becoming more and more degenerate. My life was spinning out of control. I didn't really know who I was. At the time, all I knew was that I was disenchanted and had to get out."

Nita was afraid of the "mess" she had become. "I was pretty miserable with who was I associating with and who I was." So she stopped doing drugs of all kinds. She even cut back her drinking to just social drinking. But that wasn't enough to fix a greater problem: "I hated myself and didn't see anything remotely good about myself." On top of everything else Nita was dealing with, she got pregnant and delivered her first child, a son.

"When I got pregnant and had my first child, everything began to change. Life wasn't all about me anymore, but I still had a terrible need to be known. To be loved and accepted just as I was. Because of the love I had for my son and the gift he was to me, I knew that he deserved the best me that I could give him, and I wasn't even close to being that person."

One night, after putting her son to bed, Nita sat down to watch TV. She paused on a channel carrying Christian programming during which a testimony was being given. Even though she wasn't paying attention to the details of the testimony, she was struck by the thought that only Jesus could save her.

"So I cried out to Him to save me from myself and the mess I had made of my life. I knew He was present with me in my home. When I reached out to the Lord, He came to me in a wave of love and peace. I can feel it now like it was yesterday. He accepted me, just as I was—totally broken, with nothing to offer Him. He directed me to a church and set me on a path of discipleship with Him."

Nita became active in the church, as did her husband, although they had separated. For Nita, this was a time of service and study. She took every opportunity to know Christ better and learn His Word more fully. And she focused on the Bible's lessons on being a parent. She was determined to be a better parent than her mother and father had been for her.

At the time of her conversion, Nita was fulfilling a dream she had had since she was fifteen. "Against my parents' wishes, I did not go to college but went to technical school to become a hairdresser." Nita loved her job. It satisfied a creative spark and gave her a chance to listen to her clients, talk with them, and, often, make them feel better about themselves.

Her efforts to be a good mother were tempered by the fact that she and her husband were separated. The mounting bills required that she find part-time work to supplement her salon income. One person who knew she was in need of a job was a fellow church member she had worked with on an "Alpha Course" Bible study. He worked for the Society of Anglican Missionaries and Senders (SAMS).

"I received a call from the director at the time, who knew me from church and as a result of working on the Alpha together. SAMS needed someone to fill a position, and he knew I was looking for part-time work. So he called me, and I interviewed and got the job. I never would have thought to do this work. I had never had office experience, and I had no missionary experience. I thank the Lord that He brought me to this place. In hindsight, I will say that God directed me to SAMS."

When the Lord was ready to choose Nita Dempsey for His service, Nita Dempsey was ready to serve Him. Her story is one of an odyssey through "the valley of the shadow of death" to fulfillment of His plan for her life through her work on behalf of those serving Him in mission fields throughout the world. And she couldn't be happier about it.

"Jubilation! I couldn't quit thanking God and telling my sons of His great provision. I came to know Jehovah Jireh."

20

KEVIN GOOD
No Soul Left Behind
Founder and Executive Director, Acts4Youth

*This is how we know what love is: Jesus Christ laid
down his life for us. And we ought to lay down our
lives for our brothers and sisters. If anyone has
material possessions and sees a brother or sister in
need but has no pity on them, how can the love of
God be in that person? Dear children, let us not love
with words or speech but with actions and in truth.*
1 John 3:16–18

Who would want to leave the cushy setting of a private
school to work with troubled teens in risky areas of a city?
Kevin Good would. And he completely understood why
he was making the move.

"Because God wanted me to get to know Him better,
become more of the person He created me to be, and help
share His love with boys from disadvantaged communities."

Kevin is in alien territory in the communities he serves.
He grew up with an extended family in a middle-class
home in a middle-class community. His parents worked
hard in blue-collar jobs. His mother "was very sensitive to
the needs of others," and his dad was active in local school
and sports leagues. "We were religious, with a Catholic
background, but were not very devout and often saw
church as an unwelcome intrusion."

As Kevin moved into his middle-school years, he began having conflicts with his parents and in his home life. He sought out, and found, the company of peers who offered him the chance to express his rebellious feelings.

"During that time, I had a sense that many of the things I was doing were wrong, but I could not find the inner strength to change."

When Kevin was in ninth grade, his brother, a senior, joined a Christian group called Young Life. Kevin saw Young Life as a chance to have fun, meet other students, and gain new friends. However, once in the organization, he found something more than the surface reasons for which he had joined the group.

"I had heard my brother and some of his friends saying they were Christians. I also noticed a change in my brother, who used to spend more time hosting parties with drinking and drugs."

The more time Kevin spent around Young Life and the other students in it, the more he became interested in learning what it meant to be a Christian.

"I soon realized it was more than being religious, that it was more about having a relationship with God through Christ. So during my ninth-grade year, I welcomed God's presence into my life, asked forgiveness, and expressed faith in Christ."

After he finished high school, Kevin attended college and pursued a degree in teaching. "I enjoyed working with kids, studying how people learn, and thought I could handle the classwork."

Once he graduated, Kevin and his wife, Anissa, moved into a wealthy community in Charlotte, North Carolina, where Kevin taught in the public school system. He also pursued his dual interests in soccer and serving the Lord in a unique program. "I served the Lord with a Christian ministry called Missionary Athletes International. They use soccer as a platform to spread the Gospel message."

Kevin taught for two years at a public school and for

one year at a private school. Well before the end of the third year, Kevin had wearied of teaching. "I would often be looking forward to summer break by Christmas time."

He also found out that he was less interested in working with students from privileged backgrounds. He was, in fact, more drawn to students from disadvantaged circumstances. The public school bused in lower-income African American students from the other side of town. These students, especially the boys, were frequently in trouble, and most teachers wished they had stayed in their own communities. "Many of the boys were difficult to manage in class, and I became frustrated with their unwillingness to comply.

"By the end of that year, my anger started to turn to compassion, and I wanted to get to know these students. I began to spend most of my spare time getting acquainted with their families and communities. The more time I spent getting to know the boys, the more my eyes and heart were opened to their challenges. I no longer saw the boys as interference with my lesson plans, but as students in need of intervention due to a multitude of challenges. I was drawn to trying to help the boys who, in most cases, were without dads and surrounded by crime, drugs, unemployment, and a lack of vision for their futures."

It was during this time that Kevin began to realize that he seemed to have an ability to see needs, create a vision, and design services to help address those needs. After three years of teaching, it was clear that the classroom was not his long-term desire. He began to seek out other ways to express his interest and talents. Each day after school and during the summertime, Kevin used his own car and finances to provide an after-school program and summer camp for many of the boys in his fourth-grade class. He tried to get local churches involved as partners and contributors. "I was disappointed to see the wealth in the churches and their lack of priority for the work of helping these boys."

Kevin quit his teaching job, stopped working with the

Soccer Ministry, and focused his attention on learning as much as he could about ministries like the one he envisioned.

"I traveled to various states to visit holistic programs that were working with African American youth in disadvantaged communities."

With no reason to return to Charlotte, Kevin followed God's lead to serve a church in his hometown, Baltimore. The only problem was that they didn't have any funding. "Still, I had a sense that God wanted me to pursue this type of work and that He would provide the resources, so I told them I would seek to raise the resources for my position."

With that commitment, Kevin began his search for funding. He didn't have to go far. Once again, God made Himself openly present in Kevin's pledge to be where the Lord wanted him to be.

"My home church, located in Ellicott City, Maryland, provided ten thousand dollars of seed money, so my wife and I moved back to Maryland before the start of the next school year. We moved into the community we were going to serve so we could better understand its needs."

In 2008, Kevin began the process of putting into place the physical reality of his call from God. He sought out his friends for help, and one provided in a way that was vital to his plan. "The administrator at a local elementary/middle school invited me to start the program there." So Kevin did. He called the newborn not-for-profit Acts4Youth, so named for the call to action in 1 John 3:18.

Today, Kevin's response to God's call is at work and highly regarded in the city it serves. According to the Research/Marketing Group at Loyola University, "Acts4Youth is one of the only Christian organizations, if not the only one, offering solutions to at-risk boys through after-school and summer academies that address academic, social, emotional, vocational, and spiritual needs across elementary, middle, and high school."

And that's what God had in mind when He called

Kevin out of that cushy setting. He knew that Acts4Youth would be acts for Him and that it would fulfill His desire that no child should be left behind spiritually.

21

BILL LOHMEYER
Had It All—Something Missing
Missionary, Lutheran Church, Missouri Synod (LCMS)

Jesus looked at them and said, "With man this is impossible, but with God all things are possible."
Matthew 19:26

"As early as I can remember, I had the misconception that there was a perceived materialistic measure of success in life. High-paying job, big house, nice vacations, and keeping up with the Joneses would bring happiness."

Bill Lohmeyer understood the goal, and he committed himself to realizing it. He earned his bachelor's degree in industrial engineering and a master's degree in manufacturing management from Penn State. He was happily married to a fellow graduate, Nicole, and they had two young daughters. He had a good job with a large technology company. His employer was pleased with his work and treated him well. He was realizing his childhood perceptions of success.

"We had a house on a cul-de-sac, new car, 401(k), and so on. The type of things that seem so normal in the United States. I thought everything looked good on the outside, but I had a nagging sense that something was still missing from my life."

And he was right. The problem was that he didn't know what was missing. He recalled that he had had the same feeling in high school and actually had a desire to look for the answer in the Bible. But at that time, his faith was mostly limited to Sunday-morning church services and saying the Lord's Prayer before bed. "It was a check-the-box approach to being a Christian. The fact was that I was more interested in what my peers thought of me than what God thought of me."

When Bill went off to college, he reversed the usual trend of falling further away from any childhood religious experiences and feelings of faith. He became more interested in church. Eventually, he began going to church—not because his parents wanted him to but because he wanted to. His faith continued to grow after his marriage to Nicole.

"Nicole and I joined a nurturing church home that stressed reading the scripture and making God's Word part of our regular lives, not just on Sunday mornings. Jesus's teachings have a wonderful way of making us continually reflect about how we should live our lives in a pebble-in-my-shoe kind of way."

Bill was particularly taken by the messages he saw in the Parable of the Talents. It spoke to him with two important lessons. The first was that it is God who provides for us and gives us the talents we have. The second lesson was that "We are stewards, not owners, of those gifts, and He holds us to task to use them wisely because we can, and should, put them to use for God's glory." This new sense of God's gifts and our responsibility for using them helped Bill start to lessen the greed in his life.

"I needed to learn to place more value on people and relationships. Having grown in the Word and gradually easing those long-held perspectives on the perceived importance of material wealth made me wonder, 'What am I doing with my talents?' I would often wonder about this while spending countless hours trudging around the yard with a tank sprayer, trying to keep my grass pristine. 'Is this really my calling in life and the best use of my time?'"

A month-long job assignment in Africa caused Bill to see the contrast between the business world's ideas of esteem, money, and wealth and the example Christ gives us. It often nudged Bill to rethink the childhood question, "What do I want to do when I grow up?" He had often thought of possibly retiring early and devoting much of his time as a retiree to charitable work. But then the unexpected death of Nicole's father brought to light a new perspective.

"What am I waiting for? If serving the Lord full time is something I really want to do, what is holding me back? Life is fragile. What if I don't make it to retirement age? I don't want to regret not doing something that's a life goal. I couldn't come up with a better answer in my mind than that I wasn't fully trusting in the Lord to provide for me."

Bill knew he had to get his priorities straight. He needed to remove the burden of trusting in himself, and instead, trust in the Lord to provide. Part of that process was aligning his life goals with his work goals. Bill understood that it was basic nature to think that we are the ones in full control of our lives. But he saw an example of how that just wasn't so when he found himself in need of surgery.

"The thing that made me most anxious was how the general anesthesia would take away my sense of being in charge. Rather, I had to trust in the medical professionals to see to my well-being. How much more must we look to our Creator and know that He is the potter and we are the clay. Once I realized there was nothing to hold me back from missionary service, Nicole and I started to listen less to what the world tells us is important and listened instead to how the Spirit was calling us."

Bill and Nicole sought to learn more about the mission work of the Lutheran Church, Missouri Synod (LCMS). They knew they each had skills and experiences they could put to work for the Lord on the mission field. They felt a pull to service opportunities in the Dominican Republic. Within two years, the Lohmeyer family began their mission work. With that, they built a new life in the Dominican Republic.

The LCMS in the Dominican Republic has several focal areas, including sharing the Gospel, church planting, mercy ministry, and training new workers for Christ. For example, the Lord has used his servants to build and oversee a group home for youth with disabilities. They receive personal care they otherwise would not have access to. But there's more. "These children now know of Jesus's love and the salvation He brings."

Proclaiming the Good News is always the first priority of the mission team. But they also bring with them skills for more practical needs. Bill finds ways to work in mercy ministry projects, such as the group home, finding ways to sustain the mercy projects for the long term, and building projects. "Nicole uses her background in teaching to improve the mission's day school and to help the teachers on teaching methods and improving literacy." And "Our two daughters enjoy telling others about Jesus."

Bill is not so certain that his work in the Dominican Republic sets Nicole and him apart from any other Christian. "We can all be missionaries in our everyday lives." He points out that the scriptures are full of God using sinful people to be His instruments. I think God calls us to serve Him in different places and capacities, regardless of background and skills." He points to Matthew 19:26 and notes that it says, "With God all things are possible."

"This verse reminds me that I do not walk this life alone, but rather I can place my trust in God through good times and bad and know that His steady hand will guide my path. Though I may step well away from my comfort zone, I know God will use me to do things I could never accomplish on my own."

What no technology, not even Google Earth or its successors, will ever be able to show is that Bill is right. He is not walking alone.

22

SCOTT BAILEY
Two Roads Diverged
Hospital Chaplain and Priest

> *But when the kindness and love of God our Savior*
> *appeared, he saved us, not because of righteous things*
> *we had done, but because of his mercy. He saved us*
> *through the washing of rebirth and renewal by the*
> *Holy Spirit, whom he poured out on us generously*
> *through Jesus Christ our Savior.*
>
> *Titus 3:4–6*

In Robert Frost's wonderful poem "The Road Less Taken," he writes of coming to a divergent point in the road he was walking. He has to choose one path to follow. As he makes his choice, he writes, "Oh, I kept the first for another day!"

In contrast, Scott Bailey writes the following of his choice of the two paths facing him as he sensed God's call: "If I did not take definitive steps to obey His call then, I was never going to do it. At the time, I was seriously exploring the possibility of going into business for myself. What I clearly sensed at the moment was that I needed to choose which road I was going to travel in life."

Scott understood that for those who choose to follow God's path to full-time Christian service, there is no keeping the unchosen path "for another day." God's vocational path requires a complete commitment that Scott first recognized in March 1996. He was on a ten-day construction mission trip to Santa Cruz, Bolivia, when the fork in the road was laid before him.

"One early morning when I was alone in my room praying before heading to the job site for the day, I had a clear sense that God was speaking to me. What He was saying was clear. First, God was calling me to full-time vocational ministry. Second, I was to relocate to attend seminary." And the final piece of the message? "The moment for decision had come."

The decision was not easy. There was another clear and comfortable path for Scott. It was the successful career track he was already on. "In college I majored in business administration. I kind of stumbled into my first career, a management position in the plumbing and heating industry. I learned the business both 'in the field' and then later, on the office and management side of things. After moving 'inside,' I worked as an estimator and project manager."

Scott grew up in an era-classic family. His father worked, and his mother focused on raising the children. He had a younger sister. "From my earliest recollection, my family was always active in church." Their church trended toward a more liberal theological position on matters of faith. A clear presentation of the Gospel was not a part of Scott's early ecclesiastical education. The church was also weak in maintaining a consistent youth ministry. Where there should have been a fulfilling Christian experience, there was a vacuum. But that was to change in his early teens.

"My journey to a living faith relationship with Christ began as I started high school." A group of Scott's friends attended another church, of the same denomination, but with a more active youth ministry. Their church was also closer to his home, so he began to spend more time with them.

"It was through members of this youth group and the wonderful pastor of that church that I came to understand the Gospel and my need to fully commit my life to Christ." Scott did just that. The work circumstances Scott found himself in didn't make it easy all of the time. But God was using that time and that situation to prepare Scott for the future.

"In some instances, these folks were more than a little 'rough around the edges,' and in many cases they had little or no exposure to genuine Christians or Christianity. The people I connected with, and the relationships God helped me build, were just as much a ministry as what I am doing today. Most significantly, these experiences helped me to better understand the struggles, challenges, and joys known by so many people in everyday life."

Scott better understood the people he would one day serve, and the Lord was ready for him to be His vocational servant. Scott, of course, was always ready to serve the Lord. But as a vocation? Not yet.

"Quite frankly, I ran from the call for a long time."

As Scott looks back now, he believes he was being called as early as high school. But the issues he had with the church of his youth still caused him to "dodge the reality that God was calling me to full-time vocational ministry." So he continued working in the construction industry, remained active in his worship life, and stayed involved in the ministries of his church. "I was also quite involved in the leadership of a local parachurch ministry, where I led a weekly Bible study and eventually served on the board of directors."

From time to time, Scott explored the possibility of a vocational ministry with his pastor and friends who were already in the ministry. And he would explore the options for further education in Christian service. All part of the journey in God's plan. He was still single, so his decisions were his alone…and God's.

Then came the Santa Cruz experience. "My reaction

was a clear and settled sense of what I needed to do. I was thirty-one years old at the time, and I knew what God was saying as clearly as I ever have in my life. I had a settled sense of peace."

Although Scott wasn't excited about leaving his career, his family, and the area he had lived in his whole life, he was excited to be taking the steps that would "more fully equip me for the work to which God was calling me...that would set the trajectory for the rest of my life."

At the time of his calling, Scott was a member of the Assemblies of God. So he sought out entry to a church-associated seminary. In 2000, he graduated with a divinity degree. That alone would have made it a special year. But following graduation, "I married my wonderful wife, Tammy." Together, they served as staff pastors of a church and planted a new church in a neighboring community. While serving his new congregation, he also became involved as a volunteer chaplain at the local community hospital.

"The invitation to serve as a hospital chaplain opened the door for a whole new realm of ministry for me." Scott intensified his training for hospital chaplaincy and completed a residency for this specific ministry in 2009. The hospital at which he had completed his residency was a regional Level I Trauma Center. Scott was assigned to be the Trauma Service resident chaplain. "Doing ministry on the Trauma Service was a wonderful, but also incredibly intense, experience."

It was during this same period that the Lord led Scott and Tammy to make the transition from the Assemblies of God, "which we still love," into the Anglican Church in North America (ACNA). In 2014, Scott was ordained as an ACNA priest and assists at an Anglican church in Virginia while continuing his hospital chaplaincy.

"I simply marvel at the grace of God that He would call me to serve as a priest in His church. It really is all by his grace and mercy. The longer I live, the more profoundly aware I become of this reality."

"Two paths diverged..." And, by God's grace, Scott Bailey chose the right one.

23

BOB KIMMEL
Holding the True Key
Prison Chaplain

Though I am free and belong to no man, I make
myself a slave to everyone to win as many as possible.
1 Corinthians 9:19

"God has called me to be a hope dispenser to those who have lost all hope. I let men and women know that they can be reconciled to God and have that same peace and purpose in life that I received over three decades ago."

There was nothing in Bob Kimmel's childhood to indicate that he might be presenting the message of Christ as Savior to anyone. "I was raised in the Jewish faith." Bob was the son of two loving parents, Nelson and Nettie Kimmel. "I have very good memories of my childhood."

When Bob entered his teen years, he rebelled. It was a perfect time for rebellion—the 1960s. "All that came in with that decade and the next was available for me." Even as he rebelled, Bob sensed that something was missing. He felt an intense desire to search for the truth. "I studied all the major religions of the world. Nothing seemed to satisfy my thirst."

By this time, Bob had begun a career in the landscaping business. Beginning in landscape maintenance, he worked in various areas of the discipline, including design, garden-center management, and for a while as owner of his own landscaping company. Even as he worked in an area of comfort and enjoyment, Bob's curiosity about a source of "truth" left him unfulfilled. "I was still dry on the inside." But that was about to change.

"One day I was transplanting some landscape plants at a local nursery, and a gentle giant named George Herring asked me if I would accept a Gideon's New Testament. I did and thanked him for it. I thanked him many times, for this was the beginning of the end. This was when my search would finally be over and I would find the truth."

Still, there were "many turns and many rough waters" before a March evening in 1979 when Bob would finally feel the true power of Christ in his life. By then he had married. One evening he and his wife, Margaret (Marge), went to their church to watch a Christian film called *Distant Thunder*. After the film was over, their pastor shared the Gospel with attendees. As Bob heard the words of the Gospel, something happened to his heart. It was opened, and the words from the Bible made "more sense than anything else I had ever heard before."

Bob and Marge walked back to their car. It was the walk of a lifetime.

"I sat for a minute crying and then slowly turned to her and said, 'Honey, I've come home.' I felt a ton of weight lifted off of my life. It was my sins. A joy that swept over me that was indescribable. That night I repented and trusted Jesus Christ as my Savior."

Bob was now a Christian working as a landscaper. As he continued his work into the 1990s, a "holy uncomfort" gripped his soul. He didn't know what was going on. He was a miserable man until one life-changing night.

"Alone in my office in prayer and reading the Bible, I yielded to God and surrendered to His call into the ministry." Bob was ordained as a pastor in a nondenominational Bible church in 1996 and accepted a call to the Uniontown Bible Church in Uniontown, Maryland. Bob describes the result of fulfilling his desire to "be obedient to the Lord as giving him joy and peace."

"I have always sensed the nudge in my heart to serve the least, the lost, and the lonely of the world. God used me to touch the lives of the homeless in Baltimore City, the aged and forgotten at a local nursing home, the middle-school kids as a youth leader with my wife Marge for years, and also those who are in prison. I served these men and women as a volunteer for more than twenty-five years before being called to the same detention center in Carroll County to serve as its chaplain."

Now ministering to sinners behind bars, Bob has the same message to those he served on the outside. "I let men and women know that they can be reconciled to God and have that same peace and purpose in life that I received over three decades ago."

Today, his career might seem far removed from the man planting flora and fauna in the yards of his clients. But not to Bob. "God uses all things in our lives. You see, it's all about relationships. Everyone you meet this side of heaven is loved by God and needs to know this and be pointed the way home."

The man who once felt a "holy uncomfort" with his life today helps spiritually restless prisoners at the Carroll County Detention Center find a place of holy comfort. And he does it with one uncomplicated message: "God loves us and sent His one and only Son to prove this perfect love to us on the Cross. And He placed the exclamation point that He meant it when He rose from the dead three days later. By God's grace, each and every person, here and all over the world, can come to Him and be saved."

Bob Kimmel chose 1 Corinthians 9:19 as the scripture verse to precede his story: "Though I am free and belong to no man, I make myself a slave to everyone to win as many as possible."

Now that we know Bob's story, we have to ask, how could he have chosen any other verse?

24

RANDY NEASE
A Tough Call
Methodist Minister

*For we know that all things work together for good
for those who know God, who are called according to
His purpose.*

Romans 8:28

"Even at a young age, I was told by a godly black maid, Euella May Gardener, who worked for us that I would one day grow up to be a preacher. That stayed with me through the years, I guess." Ms. Garner was right. But Randy Nease spent a good number of years trying to prove her wrong.

Randy was raised in the small town of Port Wentworth, Georgia, by good Christian parents who played a strong, active role in the lives of their five children. Love and affection were shown openly in the home. "Everything was simple, relaxed, and laid back." Randy's mother raised her children to believe they could do anything they set their minds to do. It was a lesson Randy took with him for the rest of his life.

The family was active in their church. If the church doors were open, they were there. Randy's parents loved the Lord and were not afraid to share their convictions. What should have been a strong set of positive influences in Randy's life had just the opposite effect.

"I resented being made to go to church, and I thought my parents were boring compared to all my friends' parents. I wanted to enjoy life, and living at home was choking my lifestyle."

In Randy's junior year of high school, he began experimenting with alcohol and drugs. He would frequently sneak out of the house to go get drunk, then sneak back in with the help of one of his younger brothers. On one particular night, shortly after he had graduated from high school, his father met him on the other side of the window. Randy had been told many times that as long as he lived at home, he would have to follow the rules of the house. And the one rule that was never to be broken was coming in drunk. Randy's father confronted him, and an ugly scene ensued. It meant nothing to a completely inebriated Randy.

"The next morning, my dad came into the room and told me he wanted me out of the house by the afternoon."

What might have been a devastating edict to another young man was to Randy a "Get Out of Jail Free" card. He saw it as an opportunity to live his life without being told what to do. He moved in with some friends and found a "halfway decent job" and "jived." He hadn't been on his own long when the railroad put out a notice that it was hiring. Randy had always dreamed of working for the railroad. "When I was a little boy, I went on a train ride in kindergarten. They let me sit in the engineer's seat, and I was hooked. From that point on, that's all I thought about."

After several weeks of interviews, Randy was hired as a fireman, an engineer in training. "My first month's paycheck paid me more money than my dad was getting. I began to live the life. I started buying all the things I thought a successful single man should have. I bought a red 1967 Corvette and a beautiful home. I partied like there was no tomorrow. There was no one to tell me what time to come home, no one to tell me what I could or couldn't do."

It all seemed like a dream come true—hard partying and excessive drinking. He even had a standing charge account at a nearby liquor store. Randy had most young men's dream...a life filled with partying and girls.

But Proverbs 22:6 says, "Train up a child in the way he should go: and when he is old, he will not depart from it." Randy's parents had brought him up in the right way, and no matter how hard he tried, he couldn't run away from "it." He would find himself faced with old family friends who would witness to him. It would make him feel bad and angry. As hard as he tried, Randy couldn't run away from God. God was always there.

"I can't tell you how many times the words of that godly black woman rang in my ear: 'You are going to be a preacher one day.'" It seemed a complete misfire in the face of his current reality.

Then one day, the music stopped, and Randy's partying days came to a screeching halt. Randy was water-skiing. Both he and the driver of the boat had been drinking. "That's the last thing I remember." The driver got too close to the dock, and Randy ran into a pole at forty miles per hour. Had someone not acted quickly and pulled Randy out of the water, he would have drowned. "I have no doubt my soul would have been bound for hell."

Randy woke up in a hospital with a skull fracture from his hairline to his eyebrow. The impact jarred the optic nerve. "I remember the first time I opened my eyes and the horror of not being able to see. The first thing that went through my mind was, 'I will never be able to see again.'"

The next day is one Randy describes as "one I will never forget." People came by all day long to visit. Not Randy's friends, but friends of his parents. He didn't know them, and he couldn't see them. "But this is what they said: 'You don't know me, but I'm in your mom and dad's prayer group, and I have come to pray for you.' People who didn't know me! People who would take time out of their schedule to pray for someone they had never met."

That night, Randy was lying in his hospital bed. He was alone in his room when he felt the presence of someone at the foot of his bed. "A voice called out and said, 'Do you need help?' It frightened me, so I never answered it."

Several days later, Randy was released, but he still couldn't see. "My mom and dad took me home with them. After all I had done to them and how I had avoided them, they still took me home."

One night as Randy lay in bed, he felt a darkness come over him like he had never experienced before, and he knew it was Satan. He recalled the words his mother had said to say if he ever felt like Satan was taking control of his life. Randy yelled out, "Satan, I rebuke you in the name of Jesus Christ, and I command you to leave me alone! Then I heard a voice, the same voice I heard in the hospital, and it said, 'You called, and I am here.' At that moment, I knew Christ was real. I knew He was in my life and things would be different. That was the night that changed my life forever."

Randy recovered, fully regaining his eyesight and returning to his job. And things did change. In time he was promoted to engineer. His childhood dream had come true. "It was a wonderful job. I enjoyed working with the railroad so much I would sit by the phone to get the call to run the train. No one could have enjoyed their job more."

But being happy with his railroad career was not the change the Lord had in mind for Randy. He had another message for him, and it was going to be delivered with an impact equal to the first.

One morning as Randy was riding a shuttle bus to pick up a train, a car ran into the shuttle. Randy's kneecap was torn off. He was out of work for nearly a year. Randy's new bride, Bernardine, became their sole source of support as a teller. Going from his salary of $35,000 a year as an engineer in 1976 to her $7,500 a year as a teller was no small thing. While Randy was recuperating, his wife's pastor asked him to consider filling the spot of youth worker until Randy could return to work. Randy prayed about it and felt led to accept the role.

"From the day I started, I knew this was where I really needed to be. When I did start back to work with the railroad, I found myself not enjoying it. I dreaded the phone calls to go to work because church is where I really wanted to be. As time passed, I felt God calling me to ministry."

At first, Randy fought the idea because he made such good money with the railroad. In fact, he had a great suggestion for God. If he stayed with the railroad, he could minister to all the sinners he worked with and still make the good money he was making. "That idea didn't go over well with the Lord. God keep tugging at my heart to tell me He wanted all of me."

In 1978, Randy Nease left the career he thought he loved most. He and Bernardine moved to Valdosta, Georgia, where Randy took a small country church making—you guessed it—$7,500 a year.

Today Randy is senior pastor at Trinity United Methodist Church in Pooler, Georgia, in the career he loves most.

"It's all unusual and pleasingly strange. But God's Word says, 'My ways are not your ways, and my thoughts are not your thoughts.' That pretty well sums it all up!"

Euella May Gardener knew that way back then.

25

PAUL CHRISTIAN
For the Beauty of the Creator
Lutheran Minister

So do not fear, for I am with you; do not be dismayed, for I am your God. I will strengthen you and help you; I will uphold you with my righteous right hand.

Isaiah 41:10

"You could say I had a bucolic childhood—a cross between *Mayberry RFD* and *Little House on the Prairie*."

You could say that, indeed. Paul Christian grew up on a farm in southwestern Minnesota just eleven miles from Walnut Grove, the town of *Little House on the Prairie* fame. "On our farm we milked about ninety cows, raised hogs and at times sheep, chickens, and horses. The two main crops we grew were corn and soybeans with some alfalfa, wheat, and oats." The oldest of Darrell and Mary Christian's five children, Paul was surrounded by an extended loving family so close in proximity that after-church trips to see his grandparents were a Sunday routine. "We went to two family reunions every year."

Paul was an active member of the local 4-H club, the Garvin Hi-Fliers, and the Future Farmers of America. He showed and judged livestock. In school, he was equally as active playing football and wrestling, as well as being a member of both the school concert and marching bands, playing a tuba for one and the sousaphone for the other. And to top it off, he and his siblings all marched in the Box Car Days parade, once taking the Best Costume Award. "Mom had taken boxes and cut out the tops and bottoms and took twine string and made shoulder straps so we could carry the boxes as we walked inside of them. She decorated the boxes to look like trains with an engine and a caboose with the slogan 'Box Car Days: Fifty Years of Fun.'" It was truly the Mayberry of Minnesota.

In addition to all of his other activities, Paul was very involved with the Lutheran church, especially Luther League. It was an active league, even conducting the sunrise services every year for the church. During his junior and senior years of high school, Paul wrote and preached his own sermons. His pastor encouraged him to go to seminary, "but at that time, I wasn't sure if I wanted to be a dairy farmer the rest of my life, and I hated school. So I did the most logical thing and joined the US Air Force." During his tour of duty, Paul was introduced to his first career—carpentry. Woodworking was not an alien discipline. He had taken woodworking classes in high school, even "building wooden folding chairs and an oak hope chest lined with cedar that won reserve champion for woodworking exhibits at the county fair."

It was while Paul was stationed at Pease AFB in Portsmouth, New Hampshire, that he became active in Holy Trinity Lutheran Church. He and the pastor, Rev. Earl Werdelin, developed a friendship. One day, Paul asked Rev. Werdelin about the prospect of his becoming a minister. He advised Paul to "fight it until you can't fight it anymore." So the fight was on. But only gently, for then.

Paul spent part of his service time at Osan Air Base in Korea assigned to the 554th RED HORSE Squadron. It was while he was on Temporary Duty (TDY) at Hickam AFB in Hawaii that he reenlisted. It was not just any reenlistment ceremony. It took place at the site of the Arizona Memorial. And he was the only reenlistee there.

But there was more. At the end of the ceremony, Paul's commander presented him with the flag that was flown at the memorial during the ceremonies. "It was probably the most memorable experience of my USAF career."

Paul's next assignment was in Florida at Elgin AFB. It was while he was stationed there that three major events changed his life. The first was the decision to begin working on a college degree. The second was meeting and dating Sharon Russell, a local property manager. They met at Good Shepherd Lutheran Church. That church turned out to be a special place in their lives. They met there and then, in 1992, they were married there. In time, they would return for a final visit.

The third event was leaving the Air Force. "I had planned to make the Air Force a career proposition. But my brand-new Ford Ranger truck was rear-ended at a stop sign by a Mustang going eighty-two miles-per-hour. The accident was so bad that they had to cut the top off of my truck to get me out. I required spine fusion surgery. That ended my military career ambitions."

After his Air Force tour, Paul eventually found work with the US government in a job that perfectly suited his training. "I used the same skills I learned in the USAF when I worked for the National Park Service from 1997 to 2007 at Little Big Horn National Monument on the Crow Indian Reservation in Montana and at the Petersburg National Battlefield near Petersburg, Virginia." Sharon once again found work as a property manager.

Life in Petersburg was good. Their lives were active, they made friends, and they felt comfortable that it was "home." But life for them was to change radically. In October 2000, Sharon was diagnosed with melanoma cancer. Over the next fourteen months, she battled the disease with valor. But her condition worsened, and it became apparent that she would lose. But only the earthly fight.

"Sharon saw death as a part of life, so she accepted it

with a sense of peace. Even as her health was wasting away, Sharon reminded us that she was alive with Christ and would be for eternity."

On Thanksgiving Day 2001, at the age of thirty-four, Sharon joined "the great cloud of witnesses who had gone before…" The memorial service was held in the same church where they met and were married only nine years earlier.

"There are times when I have availed myself to God, getting out of the way and stepping back, trusting and believing in God's promise of providence." For Paul, this was one of them.

In December, Paul returned to Virginia and once again became an active member of Our Redeemer Lutheran Church. He served as an usher, teller, and lay assistant, serving communion. He taught adult Sunday School and Vacation Bible School and sang in the choir. He gave temple talks and represented the congregation at the Synod Assembly in Roanoke. In the pastor's absence, Paul wrote and delivered his own sermons.

In October 2002, not quite a year after Sharon's death, Paul decided to take a vacation. He was driving down to the Outer Banks of North Carolina when something told him that he needed to be in church that morning. "But I wanted to go to the beach. I drove back and forth on the road several times until I finally gave in and went to church." The "something" was God. He had a plan. "The moment I walked into church, I saw Dee Ortiz, a fellow congregant. It was only the second time I had seen her, but I remembered her name and said, 'Hi, Dee.' We walked to Sunday School together and sat down beside each other."

On June 28, 2003, Paul and Dee were married. "We haven't been apart since then."

There was still an unresolved issue in Paul's life: God's will for his true calling. Remembering Rev. Werdelin's words, Paul fought the idea of the ministry until "I finally came to the point I could not fight it anymore and started looking into seminary."

Paul's time of discernment was coming to a close. "My fight against the ministry ended when Dee and I attended a seminary weekend retreat at the Lutheran Theological Seminary at Gettysburg (LTSG) in Gettysburg, Pennsylvania. Dee and I knew this was the place God was calling us to be."

Paul now knew where God wanted him to be and what He wanted him to do. But there was one more significant hurdle. "I had my own insecurities at first about the amount of work and effort needed to obtain a Master of Divinity, but once I started the process, God paved the way for answering His call."

God even provided for what looked like the insurmountable costs of seminary. With the help of scholarships, one from his home church, the Lutheran Church of Our Redeemer, and Dee's income, Paul was able to "finish seminary without any debt." Then, on June 4, 2011, on the same day he was ordained at the Virginia Synod, Paul received a letter of call to his first pastorate, the Lutheran Church of Our Redeemer. He was installed on June 26, 2011.

Today, Paul and Dee and their two daughters, Elizabeth and Emily, live in Petersburg. They live in the same house they lived in when he worked for the Park Service and Dee worked at Ft. Lee. They worship at the same church they left when they headed for seminary, the Lutheran Church of Our Redeemer. Only today, the Rev. Paul Christian is the pastor.

"I believe I have been tried and tested, and I am still able to believe and trust in the promises of God, and I like to share that with other people. It's not that I am anything special or better than they are but that I am an example of what God can do if we allow Him and open ourselves up to His presence and the gifts of love, forgiveness, and acceptance that God offers freely to all people, without regard to who they are or what they may have been or done."

Paul Christian knows the Lord. He has seen His work in the beauty of nature. And he has felt His faithfulness in the transitions of his life. The result: "I love to tell the story of Jesus and His love."

26

LARRY D. ANDREWS
Partnering with God
President and CEO, Partners International

*He went to Nazareth, where he had been brought up,
and on the Sabbath day he went into the synagogue,
as was his custom. He stood up to read, and the
scroll of the prophet Isaiah was handed to him.
Unrolling it, he found the place where it is written:
"The Spirit of the Lord is on me, because he has
anointed me to proclaim good news to the poor. He
has sent me to proclaim freedom for the prisoners and
recovery of sight for the blind, to set the oppressed free,
to proclaim the year of the Lord's favor."*

Luke 4:16–19

"I love that Jesus is always specific, personal, intimate, planned, intentional, and purposeful with His followers for the sake of His Kingdom. One thing that often differentiates Christ followers is how personal and intentional we are to press into Jesus to receive what He has for us and our willingness to obey what He shows us and is calling us to."

Larry Andrews didn't always know that, even though he was brought up in a moral, churchgoing home that was very stable and loving. He was one of five siblings and has an identical twin. His father was very committed to the family and limited his career growth intentionally so that the children grew up in the same house, in the same community, in Sacramento, California. His Roman Catholic family went to church every Sunday, and the children all took catechism classes, celebrated their First Communion and Confirmation, and followed all the precepts of the church. It was a family standard.

"I loved my parents and had great respect for them. I went to church every week of my life until I left for college. But my church experience was unfortunately pretty empty, and pointless. Church was never really about God and knowing Him personally; it was about obeying and honoring my parents. When I left for college, my vow was to never go to church again. I had better things to do. My college life was going to be about me, playing football, having fun, and living life on my terms." And that's how it was.

When he was twenty-one, Larry met a woman he liked while at the university. She was a church-goer, and she asked him to join her. "My like for her was more than my disdain for church, so I went." What Larry found and experienced was a very different church and worship atmosphere. There were two thousand-plus people in an intimate worship experience, with a pastor who shared honestly and personally from God's Word. And he was surrounded with a community of believers who genuinely loved God. It was so very different from his childhood church experiences.

"I was really taken aback. I figured that these folks were either wacked out, or I seriously missed something along the way about God. I knew I was a sinner, I knew I had heart issues, and I knew I needed and wanted God in my life. I was drawn, and my heart wanted to learn more."

Larry kept going to the church, staying to himself in the back. He desperately wanted to engage in worship and have the intimacy with Christ that was being preached from the pulpit. Week after week, Larry felt "held back." Until the Sunday that would change his life forever.

"On an Easter morning in 1981, I surrendered and gave my life to Christ. Worship became an intimate part of my 'born again' story. I started a journey of worship and service, and I became a Christ follower. Within a few weeks, I bought my first guitar, became involved in a Bible study, and started serving in a ministry to share the Gospel with incarcerated youth at California Youth Authority. I quickly understood that being a Christ follower was a life of surrender, obedience, and calling to serve and give away to others the grace and love Jesus gave to me."

In addition to serving Jesus and playing football, Larry's remaining college years were spent becoming academically centered—enough that he was able to pursue and complete a Master of Business Administration (MBA) degree. Shortly after graduation, Larry joined the Procter & Gamble Company. "I had thought about going into full-time ministry when I was completing my MBA program. I was very passionate to serve the Lord. As I completed my last semester, the Lord showed Himself throughout the recruiting process, and eventually through the P&G recruiting process, which I never self-selected because I did not want to leave California. The Lord spoke clearly to me when I was praying the evening of a recruiting trip I took for P&G to Cincinnati, Ohio. I recall a phone conversation with my wife, Bethanne, telling her that the Lord was revealing to me that we were going to get an offer in the morning, and we were supposed to take it."

Larry spent the next seventeen years working across various functions as a manager in the company's Information Technology (IT) division, including time spent internationally supporting a global IT initiative. In 2003, P&G decided to strategically outsource most of the IT function, and as part of that deal, Larry joined Hewlett-Packard (HP). Larry rose to become a Global Services Executive on the P&G account, where he led a $230 million business with a team of four thousand people in more than thirty countries. By every metric he was measured on, Larry Andrews was a success.

"I should have been thrilled with the success, but honestly that whole last year with HP was a struggle, and I was growing very discontented with the job. I was constantly feeling spiritual discernment that I needed to move on and that the job was significantly limiting my impact to the Kingdom."

In spite of the weight of the job and the demands on his time, Larry remained engaged with Christ in his local church. For twenty-seven years, Larry worked as a "Christian in the corporate world." Through his involvement with Sunday School and his four children, home groups, church planting, worship ministry, and benevolence ministry, Larry and Bethanne always felt they were called with a purpose to serve.

"In December 2011, after spending some extended time seeking God, I heard a clear directive from Jesus that 2012 was my last year with HP and that God was calling me to something else. Like any 'call' one gets from God, circumstances came to test my faith. About six weeks after I heard the call from Jesus to move on, I had a discussion with my VP on a Friday evening regarding some executive downsizing that was being mandated by the company. By Monday morning, I needed to name two executives to be downsized. After praying over the weekend, I came to my VP with two names, and one was mine. I used the opportunity to tell him that I was not going to be with HP by the end of the year and that the Lord was calling me elsewhere. I agreed with HP to an Early Executive Retirement program, a six-month transition plan, and I retired from HP in October 2012, feeling a bit like Abraham: 'Go to a land I will show you.'"

During the six months preceding his retirement from HP, Larry had been working with the Halftime Institute, a nonprofit, nondenominational Christian organization that "teaches, coaches, and connects marketplace leaders to help them discover and engage in their Ephesians 2:10

calling to 'the good works God prepared in advance for us to do.'" Together during this process, Larry and Bethanne integrated their hearts and calling to get "on the same page" as they moved into a new stage in their lives.

"My mission statement was clear: I felt called to serve in a global faith-based organization, with a Luke 4 ministry '...to preach the Gospel to the poor, to set captives free, to proclaim God's favor,' to leverage my international experience, and to build on my skills acquired as an executive."

What happened next should come as no surprise to those who know Jeremiah 29:11. Partners International Board decided to hire Halftime to execute a CEO search. The CEO profile made its way to Larry. "The profile was a near-verbatim copy of the mission statement I had been crafting over the previous six months. I felt the call the first time I read the profile. The experiences I had in my corporate career were what the Partners International ministry needed, and my heart was ready and shaped for service. Bethanne and I committed early in the process that we were ready to serve. When the call from the board came, we were all in!"

Today, as CEO of Partners International, Larry is using his international experience and executive skills to help reach the unreached with the Gospel. He guides the organization as it fills its mission to "build the Church in the least-reached places."

The mission is accomplished uniquely through Christ-centered, strategic, and trusting partnerships with indigenous ministries that have a vision to advance the Kingdom of God in their nations. Partners International's strategy to accomplish its mission is holistic "in word and deed." They, alongside their ministry partners, address physical, spiritual, and socioeconomic concerns with the Gospel message of hope. These partnerships can be found at work in Africa, Asia, and the Middle East in areas sometimes called the "10/40 Window" or the "Resistant Belt."

The statistics for the area Partners International reaches are expansive and impressive. The organization's reach includes sixty-eight countries that are home to five billion people. It includes seventeen hundred unreached people groups; contains the majority of the world's Muslims, Hindus, and Buddhists; and is where 80 percent of the world's poorest people live and where 85 percent are virtually unreached by the Gospel. The scope of the challenge seems daunting. But Larry is faithful. And he knows why God has placed him where he is.

"I simply love Jesus and want to do what is in His heart. I have always wanted to keep an open heart to be ready to follow. If I have learned anything from following Jesus over the past thirty years, it is that He has the very best in mind for each of us. We have every good reason to trust Him and heed His call. When He speaks so clearly, there are really no other options. You follow."

27

BARBARA DIANE ROWE
A Deep Sense of Peace
Executive Director, El Salvador Mission Team,
Christ For the City International (CFCI)

> *For God wanted them to know that the riches and*
> *glory of Christ are for you Gentiles, too. And this is*
> *the secret: Christ lives in you. This gives you*
> *assurance of sharing His glory.*
>
> *Colossians 1:27*

"I grew up as a missionary kid in a rural area of India. These formative years were key to the development of my faith in Jesus Christ and my sense of calling to live and work in other cultures."

Story over. Of course Barbara Rowe was going to be a missionary. Getting there, however, was not the straight shot it might seem.

Barbara's father was not only an ordained minister serving in the mission field; he was also an anthropologist. "He became a well-known missiologist, contributing fundamental concepts to the area of missions and how to carry out missions in a culturally sensitive and biblically sound manner." Her mother played an equally important role, both in the family's mission work and in her daughter's career. "My mother home-schooled me in the early years of my training and helped me make the decision to accept Christ in my life at a young age."

Growing up as the born-again daughter of missionaries laid the groundwork for a comfort level in Barbara's own missionary life as an adult. She was well prepared for the cross-cultural settings she would encounter. She learned to be sensitive to cultural customs, learn new languages, and understand that there are many different approaches to the human condition. She saw many of the Hindu and Muslim religious practices in India, and "it saddened me to know that the followers of those religions believe they have to make payment for their own sins, when Jesus Christ already accomplished that work Himself on the cross. Most importantly, I learned the truths as stated in the Bible, that Jesus Christ is who He claimed to be when He said, 'I am the way, the truth, and the life. No one can come to the Father except through me.'"

Barbara's family returned to the States when she was seven years old. She studied in public schools and eventually at the University of Washington in Seattle, and then at Loma Linda University in California, where she majored in nutrition and became a registered dietitian. "I wanted to have a field of study that could be used on the mission field, as well as to obtain work while living in the United States." After graduation, Barbara worked for a year in a Los Angeles-area hospital.

During her time in Seattle, Barbara had married and given birth to a daughter while working in her church to help refugees, first from Cambodia and then from El Salvador. The challenges of marriage caused Barbara to stray from her faith, and she "struggled to maintain my focus on God." While working with the Salvadoran refugees and hearing their stories, she felt God was calling her and her family to live and work in El Salvador.

So, with her husband and daughter, she moved to San Salvador to work with a local church under the auspices of the Mennonite Central Committee. They remained there for five years, experiencing the civil war and the eventual end of the war in 1992 with the signing of the Salvadoran

Peace Accords. On returning to the States, Barbara worked as a dietitian, eventually joining one of the world's most prestigious hospital systems, Johns Hopkins.

The ensuing years were the classic "best of times, worst of times." Barbara's career was a success. She moved seamlessly from her dietitian job into the management stream, first as a Clinical Manager and eventually as Director of Quality Management at Johns Hopkins Bayview Medical Center.

But the pressures of her professional life, combined with troubles in her marriage and a failure to stay close to the God she loved so much, caused her personal life to fall apart.

"I went through a divorce that affected not only me but also my fourteen-year-old daughter."

Barbara later met, and married, "a wonderful Christian man who ministered as music director and organist at the church my daughter and I were attending." Things seemed to be, once again, settling down in Barbara's life. Although El Salvador and the mission work there were still a part of her life, they were supported from a distance in spirit, by prayer, and through financial assistance.

Then tragedy struck. Five years into their marriage, her husband committed suicide. "After he died, I went through a very difficult time, dealing with grief and post-traumatic stress disorder." As Barbara was working through this time of extraordinary grief, she came to the conclusion that she really wanted to make the rest of her time on earth count for something.

"As God brought healing into my life, I felt His call back to mission work in El Salvador. I felt encouraged by this call because it gave new purpose and meaning to my life. It gladdened my heart, and I responded enthusiastically. Through the death of my husband, I had learned to depend completely on God for my provision, a lesson that proved very helpful as I entered into this renewed calling into missions."

This was a call to return to a postwar El Salvador, a country that had been unable to achieve lasting peace due to gang violence. "My background has uniquely prepared me to work in conflictive areas with a deep sense of peace that God is with me and is protecting me. But, as in the story in the third chapter of Daniel, where Shadrach, Meshach, and Abednego are about to be thrown into the fire, I say that if God chooses not to protect me, I will still continue to serve Him where He has called me to serve."

Barbara Rowe could have stayed in the United States after her husband's death. She could have stayed at her job at Hopkins, continuing to serve the Lord in a secular setting. She doesn't have to be living in a country where gang violence is daily taking the lives of so many young Salvadorans. But she believes that she is among those called to serve and preach the Gospel, sharing God's light and love with those who live in darkness.

"As director of the Faro Project, I work with local churches to encourage them to sponsor Christian youth centers in gang-controlled neighborhoods. Our goal is to reach young people before they fall prey to the promises of the local gangs, providing an alternative place for them to gain a sense of belonging, a place where they can learn about God's love and ultimately make a commitment to follow Jesus Christ. We have also begun a new ministry in the Salvadoran prison system, working directly with gang members to teach them about Jesus and His offer of redemption through the cross."

Barbara's life is a testimony that "It is not by our own power and goodness that we are able to participate in the good work that the Holy Spirit is accomplishing in this world, but rather the mercy of God and His Grace that works in us to do what is right in His sight."

Barbara Rowe: like father, like daughter. Loving God's Word. Doing God's work.

28

BRAD LAPISKA
"No" Wasn't the Answer
Pastor, Engleside Baptist Church

Unto thee O Lord do I lift up my soul. Oh my God,
I trust in thee. Let me not be ashamed, let not mine
enemies triumph over me.

Psalm 25:1–2

"At the moment God called me to serve Him, I sat up and my wife heard me say, 'No!'"

Col. Brad Lapiska had his career perfectly planned— until that moment at a church outside Marine Corps Base Camp Lejeune, when God told Brad that He had other plans for him.

A military life was not new to Brad. He grew up in a US Air Force home, and his parents were occasional church-goers. But for Brad, that relaxed approach to worship changed when he was only seventeen. His dad was transferred from his assignment in Germany to Lowry Air Force Base in Denver, Colorado. While his parents searched for a home at their new assignment, Brad spent the summer with his grandparents at their home in Maryland. He spent most of the time there hanging around with his cousin, who was very involved with the youth group at his Baptist church.

"By the end of the summer, I understood my need for salvation from my sins and trusted Christ as my

Savior." That summer also provided the added value of meeting "the girl next door," Peg Goslee, who five years later would become Mrs. Brad Lapiska.

After he finished high school, Brad attended Colorado State University, graduating in 1977 with a degree in business administration. Following graduation, he was commissioned a second lieutenant in the US Marine Corps. Shortly after that, Peg came to know Jesus as her Savior.

Believer Brad Lapiska committed to the US Marine Corps. Marine wife Peg Lapiska commits to Christ. Some year.

Brad joined the Corps and attended naval flight training. He was awarded his aviator wings in 1980 and was soon assigned to fly the AH-1 Cobra Attack helicopter. His first combat assignment would not occur until ten years later, when he was pilot of his Cobra during duty in Operation Desert Storm.

"During the next ten years, I was deployed around the world. Three of those years included two aircraft-carrier tours in the Mediterranean Sea and one infantry tour in the Western Pacific."

It was during that tour of duty that Brad became very involved in the church near Camp Lejeune, where he was stationed. At one Sunday-night service, a visiting college president preached a sermon proclaiming that America's greatest need was for "men to boldly proclaim God's Word across the land." It was that night during the service, when the preacher gave an invitation for men to respond to God's challenge, that Brad was called to preach. And it was during that service that Brad sat up and shouted, "No!"

But Brad knew that that answer wasn't final. He spent that entire night wrestling with the call, praying and searching the scriptures. He simply could not believe God would let him serve ten years in the Marine Corps, have a family, and then call him to preach. That meant leaving his career and, what's more, going to seminary. That just didn't seem to make sense. Then God spoke again.

"God put the verse from Ecclesiastes 3:1 in my head: 'To everything there is a season, and a time to every purpose under heaven.' I spent the night reading Ecclesiastes, searching for wisdom. God impressed upon me that one season was coming to a close and that He was starting a new season in my life. In the morning, I surrendered to God's will."

When Brad told Peg, she expressed her willingness, without any hesitation, to follow him wherever God led. "Her immediate support of my following the Lord was very confirming to me."

During those seminary years, he served as youth pastor to two youth groups with about two hundred teens in them. "I was blessed to see many young people go into full-time vocational ministry during those years."

After ten years of service, Col. Lapiska left active duty and joined the Marine Cobra Reserve squadron. In 1988, Brad, Peg, and their two daughters moved to Greenville, South Carolina, where Brad enrolled in seminary at Bob Jones University (BJU). However, as Col. Lapiska will tell you, there are no ex-Marines. In 1990, his unit was called up to fight in Operation Desert Storm, and he was to serve as an AH-I pilot.

"During Desert Storm, I was able to preach to the Marines in my squadron almost every week, and we saw many Marines saved."

When Brad returned to the States, he continued his studies at BJU, graduating in 1992 with a master of arts degree in pastoral studies. Two years later, the Lapiskas were called to Kansas City, Missouri, where he served as youth pastor of Tri-City Baptist Church. While serving there, Brad earned his master of divinity degree at Heart of America Theological Seminary, while Peg taught school and coached at the church's Christian school. In 1996, now ready to serve the Lord as senior pastor, Col. Lapiska was again recalled to active duty to serve as commander of a Marine Counter Narcotic Task Force. He and his team were assigned to curtail illegal drug trafficking across the Southern border of the country.

When Brad's yearlong tour of duty was over, he was called to be the Senior Pastor of Engleside Baptist Church in Alexandria, Virginia, less than twenty miles from the US capital. Perhaps you have just breathed a sigh of relief for Brad that he could now settle into a full-time ministerial position. Breathe again.

In 2003, Col. Lapiska was once again called up, this time to serve in Operation Iraqi Freedom. He served as the Deputy Marine Liaison Officer to the Combined Air Operations Center. Brad led a team of Marines responsible for integrating Marine Corps air strikes into the Master Air Attack Plan that incorporated all the air strikes of all the services and all of the countries participating in the war. Brad served in his final active-duty assignment in 2005 in a less combative role, participating in relief operations following Hurricane Katrina.

On June 1, 2006, Col. Brad Lapiska retired from the Marine Corps. But not without distinction. A chest full of decorations includes the Legion of Merit, the Defense Meritorious Service Medal, and the Strike Flight Air Medal.

"God's leadership in having me serve in the Marines before calling me to preach was unmistakably His providential leadership. During both of those combat tours, I was able to have a dynamic preaching ministry during which I saw many Marines come to Christ. All pilots have call signs and, over the years, other Marine aviators always called me 'Preacher.' Now I pastor a church right next to a military base, and the Lord has used our military background to give my wife and me a unique ministry to the military in our congregation."

Pastor Lapiska and Peg still serve Engleside Baptist Church in Alexandria, Virginia. "Our daughter, Julie, married a pastor. Our other daughter, Christina, serves on the board of a Christian school."

Engleside is located just outside Washington, DC, near the seat of the people's government Brad spent nearly three decades protecting.

"I believe God knew His plans for me while I was still in my mother's womb and brought them about in my life...guiding me forward and protecting me from consequences of some bad decisions I made when I was young. My only part was that once I committed my life to Christ, I attempted, by God's grace, to remain faithfully involved in the local church. I attended work days, I taught Sunday School, and later I became a deacon. I do believe God calls those who are already serious about serving Him."

When Col. Brad Lapiska shouted out "No!" that evening in church, it was not the final answer. God worked on him to come back with a "Yes, Sir." And in that moment, when Brad let God's plans be his plans, his faith was rewarded in ways he never imagined.

"During Veterans Day Outreach Services, both of my parents were saved at the church where I pastor. God is good all the time!"

29

JEFF FREEMAN
On the Right Track
CEO, Heritage Christian School

*Trust in the Lord with all your heart; do not depend
on your own understanding. Seek His will in all you
do, and He will show you which path to take.*
                                        Proverbs 3:5–6

"My realization was that God had prepared me for a moment such as this."

God began His preparation with Jeff Freeman when he was thirteen. It was at that young age that Jeff saw his parents accept Christ as their personal Savior. "This made a tremendous impact on me. I saw them grow in their walk and live out their faith through trials and difficult circumstances."

Jeff's encounter with Christ in his home was strengthened by hearing the Gospel in his church. And that purpose for living a Christian life was further reinforced when he began dating a young woman named Kim Sweany, who in time was to become Mrs. Jeff Freeman. "My relationship with Kim had a huge impact on my decision to follow Christ."

After his graduation from Anderson University, Jeff's career path was certain. "My first job out of college was as an auditor/CPA with Ernst & Young. At the time, it was one of the 'Big Eight' international accounting firms. I specialized in auditing clients in the insurance industry."

After four years with the company, Jeff then left to take a job as Accounting Manager at Jefferson National Life, where he worked for another four years. "I then moved on to Indiana Farm Bureau Insurance, where I worked for twenty-one years." During the two decades he was with Indiana Farm Bureau, Jeff worked in a series of ascending positions that included vice president, controller, senior vice president, chief financial officer, Senior Vice President for Development, Mergers, and Acquisitions and Strategic Planning, and finally, chief operating officer of Countryway Insurance, one of Farm Bureau's subsidiary companies.

In other words, Jeff was on a career track he seemed especially suited to, one with greater responsibility and station. Until, one day...

"I was very comfortable in my 'executive' corporate position. But the Lord started tugging at my heart that maybe there was something out there for me more ministry-related...something where I could make a bigger impact for Christ and the Kingdom of God."

While Jeff certainly felt the "tugging," he couldn't imagine that God would take him out of his comfort zone to do something ministerial. "Who, me?" He struggled with the tugging. And he prayed about it. While he was contemplating what God would have him do, the door opened. Heritage Christian School was looking for an Athletic Director to be part of its leadership team. Jeff was familiar with the institution. His wife was a teacher there, and all three of his children graduated from Heritage. He had also coached there. "I loved the school and the impact it had on my family."

But there was a hitch...or two. Although he had significant leadership experience, the job responsibilities were seemingly out of his area of expertise. The second issue was just as critical...maybe even more so. The job would require that Jeff take a large pay cut. That alone would drive most people back to further prayer. And the hope that they had misunderstood God. "The more I prayed about it, the more I felt convicted that God was providing this opportunity and calling me to it. The call was so clear and awesome."

For Jeff, it was now simply a matter of submission to the will of God. Virtually every detail involved with leaving the Farm Bureau assured Jeff that God was leading this decision and that "I needed to step out in faith to make this big ministerial transition." The interviews with Heritage Christian, the discussions with the CEO at Farm Bureau, and the financial aspects of his separation "all had God's hand on them...not to mention, He gave me 'the peace that surpasses all understanding.'"

So Jeff became the Athletic Director at Heritage Christian School. It was not the so-called "easy way out." By his own assessment, Jeff worked longer, harder hours than he had in the corporate world. In fact, after two years in the job, he was reaching the point of exhaustion and burnout. "It was just then, as I was considering other professional opportunities, that God again spoke to me with another calling." The school was going through times of crisis in both financial and nonfinancial matters and circumstances. A transition in leadership called for new management. It was God's Jeremiah 29:11 time for both Heritage and Jeff Freeman.

"I became the CEO of the school. My extensive leadership, management, financial, and problem-solving experience served me well during this time of crisis...but it was so much a God thing, and my realization was that God had prepared me for a moment such as this. This had such an impact on my faith, my calling, and my service to God...to see God at work, using an ordinary guy like me to do His work in extraordinarily challenging circumstances."

In corporate management vernacular, there is a term for not staying on the track to the top: "derailing." Fast-trackers would say that Jeff Freeman derailed. They would be wrong.

"Had I not taken the Athletic Director job at Heritage Christian School, I never would have been in position to take, or ever be considered for, the Head of School job. God used all of that...hopefully, for His glory and to move the school forward."

Jeff Freeman is on the fast track, all right. It's called the Road to Glory.

30

HARMONY (DUST) GRILLO
A Treasure for Treasures
Founder, Treasures/iamatreasure.com

And we know that in all things, God works for the good of those who love him, who have been called according to his purpose.

Romans 8:28

For some people, life is tough. Then it gets tougher. Then toughest. Until Christ makes it better. Harmony Dust can tell you about all of it.

Tough. "One of my earliest memories is of my father watching porn in the bed next to me during one of my weekend visits. I couldn't have been older than three or four. He left the state when I was five years old, and I saw him only about a dozen times throughout my childhood after that." Her mother, aware of the situation, did nothing about it. "She explained that if I wore long pants and stopped practicing my dance routines in the living room, this wouldn't be happening."

When Harmony was thirteen, her mother ran off with her boyfriend and left Harmony to raise her eight-year-old brother. "She left us with twenty dollars and a book of food stamps." To keep her and her brother in food and supplies, Harmony began stealing, always cautious to protect her little brother from any involvement in her petty theft.

"That was the summer I lost my virginity to the first boy who told me he loved me." Then her first boyfriend turned out to be number one in a successive line of people to facilitate Harmony's loss of self-worth. He was her boyfriend, source of food, security ("Anyone mess with you, I got your back"), and abuser. "And it was he who first mentioned that he could 'make money' off me."

Within two years, Harmony was giving him money from her job at the beach. After another two years, she was fully supporting him. By the time Harmony was nineteen, she was $35,000 in debt.

Tougher. "I was losing control. Young, naïve, and hopeless, I began stripping. He told me that I would only have to work for a couple of months to pay off my bills. Then I could return to a 'normal' life. I found myself trapped in the lifestyle."

By day a quiet, conservative college student, at night Harmony was another person's fantasy. "Gradually, I began to lose sight of who I was and became lost in makeup, stilettos, and the glare of stage lights. I felt fragmented and compartmentalized. My life unraveled like an episode of *Jerry Springer*."

Already feeling empty, with a declining self-image, Harmony began to use stripping as a way to take back control of her sexuality. "I finally felt like I had the upper hand. I learned to exploit for myself the very thing that men had already exploited—my body." In spite of her feelings of being in control, by day she hid her fear of recognition by hiding behind baggy clothes and sunglasses. And by clinging to a boyfriend whom she knew didn't love her. Who even impregnated another woman.

Toughest. "I thought that my life and existence were hopeless and that the relationship with my boyfriend was the only salvageable thing left. In my search for one good and pure thing, I clung to him with all of my strength and sacrificed my dignity to keep him in my life. All of my adoration, love, and worship were focused on a person who was too selfish to ever really love me."

Until Christ made it better. "I met a friend who showed me the unconditional love of God. She never tried to 'fix' or 'change' me, and her friendship with me was not contingent on my going to church with her. I never felt like a 'project.' She was not afraid of my 'messy' life. Through her friendship, I began to see an example of a woman who loved God, loved people, and loved herself."

Harmony's friend didn't lecture or give her a set of guidelines she must live by. The friend did two other things that impressed Harmony. First, she invited Harmony to join her at church. "From the moment I walked through the doors, I knew I was 'home.'" Second, the friend trusted the Holy Spirit enough to do the work in Harmony's heart. "This internal transformation is ultimately what led to change in my life and choices."

Harmony left stripping behind her. More than that, she became a witness for the Lord. "From the beginning of my encounter with Jesus, I had a sense that God was going to use my story somehow." After returning from a trip to Mozambique, where she shared her story publicly for the first time, Harmony knew that "I wanted to do work that made a difference somehow."

Once back in the States, Harmony contacted Mercy Missions, a faith-based organization with a mission to serve young women caught in a spiraling life. She wanted to know what kind of education a person would need who wanted to work for Mercy or an organization like it.

"I will never forget their response. Nancy, Mercy's founder, believes in anointing over education. 'However,' she said, 'many of the staff members here have a master's in social work.' I hung up the phone and immediately began applying to MSW programs." Harmony decided to attend the University of California–Los Angeles (UCLA).

One day, shortly before entering school, Harmony

found herself sitting in her car, across the street from the strip club where she used to work. She felt compelled to do something to reach the women still caught in "the life." God already knew that was coming. There turned out to be a stack of postcards right there in the car. They read, "Her value is far above rubies and pearls." This was exactly the message that Harmony wanted to share with the women. She began leaving handwritten notes for the women in the clubs and placing them on their cars.

"After I did this, I began to wonder if I could find a way to reach the rest of the clubs in my city and if others would want to join me. The vision of Treasures was birthed! I continued to build and run Treasures while I was finishing my master's degree."

Treasures' mission was ambitious but unequivocal:

"To reach, restore, and equip women in the sex industry and victims of trafficking to live healthy, flourishing lives and train others to do the same across the globe."

Harmony graduated from UCLA magna cum laude, at the head of her class. Shortly after graduating, she began her new career as a case manager for the Los Angeles County Department of Children and Family Services (DCFS).

"As someone who spent a brief period of my childhood in foster care, living in a group home, I found it incredibly rewarding to work with children in the foster-care system. I loved being an advocate for them and knowing that I had the potential to make a difference in their lives."

While Harmony was still working for DCFS, the story of her life was featured in *Glamour* magazine. The response to her story, and the mission and work of Treasures, was overwhelming.

"Our phone lines, website, and e-mail all crashed! My team and I worked around the clock to try to respond to everyone. I couldn't keep up with my workload at

Treasures while maintaining my full-time job at DCFS. So I took a leap of faith. I quit my job with its comfortable government benefits and went into full-time ministry."

And that is why today young women from all over the world, caught in "the life," can seek help from women who can say with veracity, "I know how you feel." It's why troubled souls can find women who can tell them, from experience, that when they accept Christ as their Savior, their sins are buried as deep as the deepest sea.

"He is a genius! If we let Him, He will take all of the threads of our past, our unique passions and giftings, and weave them all together into a beautiful tapestry of purpose!"

Harmony's complete story can be found in her
book *Scars and Stilettos*, which is available on
www.iamatreasure.com.

31

JAMES FARMER
Fr. Farmer, JD
Monsignor, St. John Catholic Church

*What profit does one show who gains the whole world
and loses his soul in the process?*

Mark 8:36

"I am the king's good servant—but God's first." Those are
the last words uttered by King Henry the Eighth's
Chancellor, Sir Thomas More. Later canonized as St.
Thomas More, he was an intensely spiritual man who was
also an eminent lawyer, literary scholar, lover of nature,
gentleman, beloved husband, and father. Truly one who
well-earned the attribute "a man for all seasons."

When the St. Thomas More Society presented its
2013 "A Man for All Seasons" award to Fr. James Farmer,
it honored a lawyer who loved law but learned to love God
first. And that commitment changed his whole life.

James came from humble beginnings. "My father was
a pipefitter; my mother worked at General Motors in the
accounting office." It was a fairly normal childhood for
young James. Youth groups, Little League baseball,
basketball, CYO weightlifting team, "lots of activities." He
and his family lived near, and attended, the local parish.
The kids went to local parochial schools—St. Clements for
elementary and Archbishop Curley High School. Just a
typical good Catholic kid.

Except for this: "I always thought of the priesthood my entire life. I suppressed it and continued to suppress it for many, many years. God was very patient with me."

When James graduated from high school, he began classes at Loyola College of Maryland, now called Loyola University, in his Baltimore hometown. While he was attending Loyola, he joined the Reserve Officers' Training Corps (ROTC), an Armed Forces officer training program. ROTC provides financial aid for students and preps them for a required of tour of duty after graduation. "We were commissioned, then graduated as second lieutenants. Forty-seven of us." Before fulfilling his term of duty, James was permitted to go to law school. The prestigious Catholic University of America Columbus School of Law in Washington, DC, was James's choice for his law studies. He was awarded his Juris Doctorate in 1972. However, entering private practice would have to wait. James still had his ROTC commitment to the Armed Services. So he joined the Army. "I served first as an officer and combat engineer, then as a general officer." In that final assignment, James was in the US Army Judge Advocate Corps. His first case provided an insight into the combined strength and passion that would mark his eventual priesthood.

It was the case of a young Spanish-speaking Puerto Rican who had been tried and found guilty. On appeal, his case was handed off to Judge Advocate James Farmer. It was his first case, and he spoke no Spanish. Recognizing the adverse effect this would have on giving his client a fair trial, James informed his commander that he could not properly defend the client. The commander insisted that the young Judge Advocate defend the man anyhow. Fr. Farmer recalls the event.

"I said, 'Sir, either you get him a lawyer who speaks Spanish, or I'll call the Secretary of the Army and report you right now.'"

James Farmer finished his tour of duty as a captain

and headed home for Baltimore, where he took a job as a Public Defender with the city. "I saw people at the depths of their humanity." It was a meeting with one of the prisoners that had a life-changing impact on James.

"I went to the jail one day and met with a particular man. His appeals had all ended, post-convictions ended. He was going to get thirty years in prison. He was about twenty years old. And he said, 'I'd better turn to God.' He said that."

James eventually resigned his Public Defender's job and went to the seminary. It was during his tenure there that James visited a priest friend. He asked the friend what he would be doing if he weren't a priest. "He said, 'I'd still be going to bars and condemning myself.' That really hit me."

And a new journey began.

It began with a visit to the nearby town of Emmitsburg, Maryland. The town hosted the Roman Catholic seminary, Mount St. Mary's. The rector there, Fr. Harry Flynn, graciously welcomed James. "The day I walked into the seminary, I knew it was where I belonged. There's this sense of peace, joy, and holiness at the Mount…it's hard to describe. It's almost palpable."

James was also impressed with the spirit of the priests he met that day.

"The priests at Mount St. Mary's Seminary were extraordinary in their holiness, wisdom, and intellect. They were extremely brilliant men, as smart as any people I'd ever met in the law profession. But they had turned their lives over."

Back home, James began to give thought to what he had witnessed among the priests. And he thought about the outcomes of the practice of law in reference to the pursuit of salvation.

"I realized after a while that the legal remedy was a very limited remedy. A person is acquitted or convicted, but the problems still continue. The legal remedy can apply only to the immediate problem you have, but the spiritual remedy that a priest can bring has eternal consequences."

After decades of studying to be a lawyer and then practicing law, James began to reassess what he was doing and where that was getting him in life...and the afterlife. "A priest brings people to Jesus and Jesus to people by bringing the sacraments to people, performing weddings, baptisms, going to funerals, and bringing the message of God to families who are grieving."

When James told his friends at the law firm about his decision to follow God's call to priesthood, the responses of his colleagues were varying and, perhaps, typical. "My boss, the Public Defender, Jim, said, 'You've been involved in some very, very difficult trials. Take a few weeks off before you do something like this.' I told one of the judges about my decision. He said, 'Is that for life?' Like it was a sentencing. I'll never forget that day."

There's another day James Farmer will never forget. In September 1976, James Farmer began formal studies for the priesthood at Mount St. Mary's Seminary. And on November 24, 1979, he was ordained, and Fr. James Farmer entered the priesthood. Today, more than thirty-five years later, Fr. Farmer serves a fourteen thousand-member congregation in a town that lies between his birthplace and Mount St. Mary's Seminary. He is also, by word and action, a strong and ever-present minister in the lives of people who have never met him—the children whose lives he saves as an ardent leader in the pro-life movement.

Fr. Farmer reflects on his call to the priesthood and acceptance to God's purpose for his life, "I don't know why He called me. But I'm very thankful He was patient."

Maybe Fr. Farmer doesn't know why God called him out of his law career into the priesthood, but he knows what God wanted him to do when he got there.

"The real joy of the priesthood is interacting with parishioners and trying to help them draw closer to the

Lord. The priesthood is all about bringing Jesus to people and people to Jesus."

32

SR. ROBIE HILLHOUSE
Up to the Challenge, After All
Director, Ministry Advancement of the Lutheran Missionary Society, Maryland; Lutheran Deaconess

> *But now, thus says the Lord, he who created you, O Jacob, he who formed you, O Israel: Do not fear, for I have redeemed you; I have called you by name, you are mine.*
>
> *Isaiah 43:1*

Roberta (Robie) Sauer Hillhouse grew up ready for God's call. And she immediately accepted it. For a while.

Robie grew up on a farm in upstate New York outside the town of Eden. "We were not rich by any material standards, but our home was filled with laughter, hard work, and involvement at the little mission Lutheran church we belonged to." Her parents, Hugh and Bertha Sauer, married and lived in Shageluk, Alaska. Bertha taught and assisted Hugh, who was a special assistant with the Bureau of Indian Affairs. At that time, Alaska was still a remote territory, so his job required that he maintain daily radio contact with the Army, doctors, and villages to share weather reports and other news. It's no wonder that Robie describes her childhood as an environment of adventure, where they were taught that they could do whatever they chose to do.

"Education, music, and literature were all important in

our family, and we were expected to do our best in school. My earliest memories include being read to after dinner. We heard everything from *Tom Sawyer* to *Chitty Chitty Bang Bang* to the poems of Robert Service. And later in the evening, the six of us kids kneeled around my mom for evening devotions and prayers. Literally at my mother's knee, I learned the Lord's Prayer, the Apostles' Creed, the Twenty-Third Psalm, and all the wonderful stories of the Bible."

Robie's mother was a strong woman and a leader. Bertha Sauer served as school superintendent at the mission church, a position often filled by men. She was the first woman to serve on the church council. As a public school teacher, she also served on the teachers' union salary negotiating team and was named "Teacher of the Year" before her retirement. Robie Sauer came from good stock, and it stuck.

"I was baptized as an infant on October 22, 1957, and was brought up as an active member of the church. I do not remember a time when faith was not an integral part of my life."

When she was sixteen, Robie felt called to "a ministry of some sort." At that time, in that place, a "call" probably meant being a teacher in a Lutheran school. And Robie knew she did not want to teach. "So I opted to go into the Navy instead of going to college. My godfather, Uncle Otto Hammermeister, spoke to my mom against this decision." As a consequence of the conversation, Robie suspended her Navy enlistment.

Robie's family was not able to pay for college. But when several churches organized a visit to a Lutheran college, she went along just to see what it was all about. On the trip, she heard about the deaconess ministry. "It was if God was saying, 'This is how.'"

So Robie followed the leading of the message and applied to the school she was visiting at the time, Concordia College in New York. However, the cost was the unyielding barrier. As He often does, the Lord provided. She was awarded a Regent's scholarship. Still, to complete her degree, Robie needed to transfer to Valparaiso University in Valparaiso, Indiana. That meant walking away from the final two years of the Regent's scholarship.

"I received several awards and student loans and worked in the summers and part time during the school year, and it became manageable."

Robie's first ministry after graduation was to a large Lutheran church in Maryland. The call was a specialized "contract" as Director of Youth and Education for three years. After that time, the call could be renewed, with or without time limits. "The position was very challenging, and I was, admittedly, naïve and young…too young. I was adjusting to living on my own, paying car and student loans. I met a young man who was to be my future husband. I was working hard to keep all the balls in the air. By the end of three years, I was unhappy with the expectations and what I felt, and still feel, were unfair judgments of my work. I married Michael, moved out of church-provided housing, and did not renew my contract."

Robie sought a job that seemed to be a good mix of math skills and valuing personal relationships. She applied for a position as a teller at a small, independent, local bank. Over the next fourteen years, she worked as a teller, customer service rep, assistant branch manager, branch manager, and assistant vice president.

Evidently, Robie's assessment of her skills was accurate. "Under my leadership, the branch grew deposits to over a million dollars, with a large portfolio of consumer and commercial loans. Later I moved to the bank's newly formed credit-card department."

During that time, Robie and Michael continued regular attendance at the church where she had been on staff. After their second son was born, they transferred to the Lutheran church just half a mile from their home. While

Good Shepherd was smaller, it still offered ample opportunities for Robie to serve.

"I was stinging a bit from my 'failure' at my first call and chose to be active as a mom and banker. As it happened, the associate pastor made some 'regrettable decisions' and was asked to resign, leaving a confirmation teaching position available. I was approached to teach and accepted."

In addition to teaching, Robie was given the opportunity to perform many ministry duties not often given to women within the Lutheran denomination. She also traveled to China for six weeks on a Teaching English As Ministry (TEAM) mission trip, followed the next year with a mission trip to teach Vacation Bible School in a remote village above the Arctic Circle.

Robie looks back at her banking days as part of God's plan for her. "I think God placed me there for my ministry wounds to heal and to regain my self-confidence. I was in a position to better serve where God was leading me next. I learned about hiring, firing, interview skills, and developed an ability to read financials and develop budgets. I also learned how tired one can be after a long day's work and longer commute. All in all, I got a clearer understanding of what it was like to work in the secular world."

Robie attributes much of the credit for staying the course through good times and bad to her husband. "Michael's unquestioning support often confirms for me that it is God's calling to which I am responding."

Today, Robie is the Director of the Ministry Advancement for the Lutheran Mission Society of Maryland (LMS), a Christian health and welfare agency providing food, clothing, chaplaincy, and "the Gospel's good news of hope in Christ Jesus" to everyone who comes to one of its ten Compassion Centers located throughout the state of Maryland and nearby York, Pennsylvania. Her responsibilities can be as varied as scraping lead paint and repainting low-income housing with volunteers from the Naval Academy to "talking to an adult Bible class about the exciting ministry of the Lutheran Mission Society."

She agreed to serve LMS for three to five years and has been with the organization for nine. "Now I am listening for God's voice as to the next place of service I may be called to."

Roberta (Robie) Susan Sauer Hillhouse knew at sixteen that God had called her to serve. Ten years later, she wasn't so sure she had heard right. So God gave her time to think about it. Then He called her again.

"I don't know why He called me to Christian service, but I am incredibly humbled that He did. It was certainly not because of anything I did or merited. Although difficult to explain, I truly do feel 'chosen'—something not of my will or choosing. Yet this feels exactly right."

33

GORDON ANDERSON
Now It Computes
Anglican Priest

Truly, God is able of these stones to raise up children to Abraham.

Luke 3:8

"The roundabout path to ordination always struck me as a bit odd, but it is not altogether uncommon, I suppose." Father J. Gordon Anderson knows about the circuitous route to answering God's call, even for those who spent their youthful years laboring in His fields.

When Gordon was a child, he attended the local Presbyterian church with his family. "We went to church every Sunday and were a pretty devout family." He attended the local public elementary school. His graduation to middle school launched him into a direction that would be life altering. Gordon's parents took him out of public school and enrolled him in a private Christian school run by the Grace Bible Baptist Church in his hometown of Baltimore, Maryland.

"It was at the Baptist school that my faith became much more personal to me. Sitting in daily Bible class impressed on me the importance of reading and studying the scriptures each day. Eventually, perhaps in about the ninth grade, I began reading the Bible every day. It transformed my life and is a habit that I continue to this day. It was at this school a few of my teachers suggested to me that I might have a vocation to full-time Christian work, such as youth ministry."

Throughout college, Gordon did get involved in ministry—in fact, a number of ministries. He sought out opportunities to serve in nursing homes and to minister through evangelism in college. He applied his spirit of ministry to his job in a Christian bookstore. The young man was a witness. He planned a future where he could use his love of the Lord. He would teach in a Christian school. Those fine plans were delayed when he "decided" he would become a pastor. But that idea never made it to the finish line. "Eventually, however, I lost interest in becoming a pastor, having decided to pursue a career in the fine arts instead. So my call lay dormant for about three years."

During the dormant years, Gordon took his first job. It was in the Information Technology (IT) business as a receptionist at Keane, Inc., an IT firm. The goal was to work there for a couple of years and then move to New York City. "All told, I ended up working there for five years, moving up the ranks to consultant on projects with the Defense Commissary Agency (DECA) of the federal government and the Department of Parole and Probation of Maryland." Gordon saved his money during the DECA years to go to New York City to pursue his career in the arts. At least, that what he thought he was saving it for.

"I had written off going to seminary altogether until I started attending an Anglican church and met their young curate who, when I told him of my previous desire to go to seminary and enter full-time ministry, said, 'Ah, perhaps God is calling you to be a priest in His holy catholic church.' Right then, at that very moment, it all came flooding back to me…like God tapped me on the shoulder and was saying to me, 'Uh, hey there. You know I have not forgotten about you. I want you to do this."

Instead of going to New York and using the money he

had saved for a career in the arts, Gordon used it to prepare for the ministry. He enrolled in St. Mary's Seminary in Baltimore. Keane generously allowed him to work part time, enabling him to put food on the table and pay his bills as he studied and prepared for ordination.

"By the time I graduated from seminary, I had dropped out of the ordination process of my church. I was disillusioned with the church and my parish in particular, where there had recently been a nasty split. I went back to working at the computer company full time."

Now unsettled, Gordon eventually left Keane. He tried his hand at teaching. It was at a parochial middle school in an impoverished section of Baltimore City, Maryland. "The job at the middle school was an attempt to be in full-time ministry, albeit, not pastoral ministry. So I still had a desire and a sense that God was calling me to the ministry, but I crashed and burned as a teacher." So Gordon tried sales in interior architectural specialties. Tired of that, he interviewed for jobs in New York. Nothing there, either. "For some reason, God wanted me to stay in Maryland in my sales job that I did not like." God knew the reason and in His time revealed it.

"A friend of mine, after her husband left her, had a nervous breakdown. I found myself taking the lead in ministering to her, praying with her, and helping her. I took that as a sign from God that He maybe still wanted me in ministry."

The incident caused Gordon to begin to reflect on all of the people who had helped him through seminary in various ways. He thought about the degree he had gotten and that he wasn't doing anything with it for God. It all seemed like a waste. "I felt as though I was being unthankful to God and the people who helped me." Gordon also took a look at the needs of the church and how so many men would love to be in full-time ministry but could not take the time to earn a seminary degree because of family commitments and other stumbling blocks.

"Yet there I was with a skill set and desire to do something for God, and I wasn't doing anything with it! When all of this hit me, I immediately got in touch with my old vocations director and asked to be brought back into the process to be ordained as a priest."

Gordon has been ordained for ten years and has served at three parishes. "My ministry has been shaped and guided by the context of the church where I served."

In Vero Beach, Florida, Gordon served a church that consisted of incredibly wealthy people who were the brightest and best of their generation. In addition to the liturgical and pastoral activities, "I taught a lot because they were brilliant men and women and very eager to learn and deepen their faith in their twilight years." Gordon also ministered to the homeless at a shelter where he spoke and played his guitar, "very odd for a high-church Anglican, perhaps."

In Blacksburg, Virginia, in his church that was two blocks from Virginia Tech, he addressed much of his ministry to the university's students. Sent to revitalize a church that was crumbling, both physically and in congregational size, Gordon spent time rehabbing the physical plant. "Our challenges were to manage a large building that was falling apart, reach college students, and attract new members. It was both exhausting and exhilarating."

Today, Gordon is serving a parish back in his home area, just outside Baltimore. It is a smaller parish that requires him to add to the routine requisites of the rector, "tons of administrative work." But the workload at St. Alban's is not what is shaping his ministry. "This is by far the hardest church that I've served because it's in a sprawling suburb. In addition, it is interracial, international, and has people of all ages. It makes it very hard to narrow my focus and decide what will work well for everyone!"

The good news? The Lord prepared Gordon for this ministry long before Gordon ever knew he would be here.

"I believe that God had me go through all of those other experiences and jobs not only because they helped me grow as a person and as a Christian, but also because they helped me in small-church parish ministry. I use every skill I learned at these other jobs every day in what I do. So yes, I absolutely believe that those jobs were also a calling from God and a way for Him to prepare me for full-time ministry."

Gordon Anderson decided he was not going to be ordained. But he forgot that God had already ordained him when he was still in his mother's womb.

34

NORMAN ENDLICH
Practice to Commitment
Director of Music Ministry

Let the word of Christ dwell in you richly, as in all wisdom you teach and admonish one another, singing psalms, hymns, and spiritual songs with gratitude in your hearts to God.

Colossians 3:16

Five-year-old Norman was sitting in his first-grade class at St. Katherine's School in Baltimore when one of the Sisters offered piano lessons to anyone who was interested. "I knew she was talking directly to me." So young Norman took the parental-consent paper home for his father to sign. That was the beginning of lessons that went far beyond the piano.

"My father is the person who taught me the most about commitment. He insisted that I practice the piano for half an hour every day after school and on the weekends. Any day that I didn't practice, he made me write one hundred times, 'I must practice the piano every day.' I continually was frustrated having to do so, but he was relentless in this pursuit, never giving up on his 'form of punishment' the entire nine years that I took lessons."

For the next three years, Norman took piano lessons from the Sisters in the convent. That was followed by another six years with a private teacher. "I got subsequent piano and music experience via playing in bands and hanging around a music store."

After high school, Norman enrolled in college at Towson University and turned his attention toward a more career-focused agenda. Four years later, he turned his degree in education into a job teaching fourth grade at schools in Baltimore County, Maryland.

Norman met his wife, then Judy Milauskas, while at Towson. He was a senior, and she was an incoming freshman. Norman was the senior orientation leader for a group of twenty freshmen, one of whom, coincidentally, was Judy. They were married in November 1969, the year Norman graduated from Towson.

Norman left his teaching career behind in December 1978 and entered the corporate world. His first job was as a technical writer and trainer with the American Totalisator Company. That job was followed by eleven other jobs in varying disciplines and management levels. "Similar to my nomadic, part-time, music career that was to come, I changed professional careers a number of times."

With the job at Totalisator, the Endlichs moved from their home in Baltimore City to the next county west, Carroll County, and began attending a different church— St. Bartholomew's Catholic Church. Coincidentally, the church was in search of an organist. A long-time friend of Judy told the pastor that Judy had played the organ at the church she had attended before she and Norman were married.

"Our pastor came to visit us and asked if my wife would be interested. She agreed, but being pregnant with our third child at the time, had to stop as the time for delivery came closer. I stepped in to take over playing the organ at the church...no questions asked."

Norman accepted the request, even though, by his own admission, he didn't know much about playing the organ and even less about playing church music. But when God is ready to use one of His servants, He provides. And prepares.

"I didn't think much about it being God's calling at the time. Little did I know how that would change."

Norman's volunteer work with the music ministry at the church ended when he accepted a new job and, once again, he and Judy moved to a town in the next county over, Montgomery County. Almost immediately, he found out that the Lord had a purpose for him there. "While talking to a fellow employee at my new job, I was informed that their church, Mother Seton Parish, was looking for a choir director. I talked with the pastor there and was hired as a volunteer, part-time choir director and accompanist for the weekend Masses, while keeping my full-time job."

As a result of growing discomfort with pastoral matters at Mother Seton Parish, Norman and Judy found a new church home, St. Rose of Lima, where he occasionally filled in for weekend Masses. When a new pastor was appointed at Mother Seton, and at the behest of many choir members and parishioners, he contacted Norman. "We had a wonderful discussion and found that our priorities aligned perfectly." As a result, Norman returned to Mother Seton. It was another step by the Lord to lead Norman to His ultimate purpose for His servant.

"I learned a great deal about Catholic music and liturgy during my second opportunity at Mother Seton from an assistant pastor who spent a great deal of time teaching me about those topics and who remains a friend to this day."

A conflation of events, including their three children's high school graduations and their scattering to colleges, led Norman and Judy to leave Mother Seton and return once again to St. Rose of Lima. He played the piano for weekend Masses but had no leadership responsibilities.

Throughout his professional career, Norman continued his education. First he completed a master of science degree in management at National Louis

University, followed by a PhD in human development at Virginia Polytechnic Institute and State University.

The nomadic nature of Norman's career brought the inevitable: another job change, another community, another parish. This time, he and Judy joined the St. Ignatius Catholic Community in Ijamsville, Maryland. Once again, Norman answered "a call" by filling in while the church sought a new choir director. Of course, he stepped into that role while he still was working full time.

For the unchurched and the churched with little knowledge of the role of a choir director, it truly is not part time, regardless of the nomenclature. Norman was working double duty.

Settled into both his job and service to his church, through the guidance of the Lord, he accepted a new job: dean of the School of Business and Leadership at Stevenson University.

"Being at Stevenson probably was the most enjoyable and rewarding of my professional jobs; however, it also was the most demanding and personally time-consuming. I decided to resign in May 2014, staying until the end of the academic year, and not having any idea what would be next for me."

Once again, God intervened to further lead Norman into service for the Lord.

"One day before I left Stevenson, I received a call from our pastor, who informed me that the latest of the music directors had resigned. He asked whether I would be willing once again to be on the search committee to find a replacement."

Norman shared the call with Judy, who suggested that he apply for the job and teach part time in an online program. In response, Norman called the pastor, and they met that afternoon. He told the pastor, "Father Mike, I don't know quite why I am here, but I have a strong feeling that I should be here. Something told me to come and talk with you and apply for the job as the music director."

In July 2014, Norman Endlich became the full-time Director of Music Ministry for the St. Ignatius of Loyola Catholic Community. And God's purpose for Norman's life was fulfilled.

"Unbeknownst to me, God always was leading the way, nudging me in the right direction to gain new skills and experiences. I truly have been blessed with the beautiful gift of music. I am equally blessed to be able to share with others through my ministry by using music as a means to foster prayerfulness and build community."

The story of Norman's response to God's call ends there. However, that was not "the rest of the story."

"I was diagnosed with oral cancer in June 2015 and underwent an extensive and highly invasive nine-hour surgery in July 2015, followed by eight days in the hospital and a weeks-long and difficult recovery period. An incredible prayer network quickly was established. Literally hundreds of prayers were offered, and myriad cards were mailed to us. The pastor and various staff members and parishioners visited during the weeks of recovery. Others provided meals and even assisted with home care when my wife had to return to work. Once I was able to attend church again, but not yet able to be at the piano, the warmth, caring, tears, and lots of hugs from our parishioners became an important and critical part of the healing process. My recent pathology results were excellent and I believe fully were the results of God's handiwork and an answer to the many prayers that were offered. And although I still have some healing to undergo from the sites affected by the surgery, I am back at work doing my music thing full time and feeling stronger and more blessed than ever."

First-grader Norman Endlich answered the Sister's question about taking piano lessons because he knew "she was talking directly to me." And so was God.

"Every time I reflect on what I am doing now and my

present, post-surgery status, I become deeply emotional. I went into the surgery experience wanting to become closer to Christ, be more prayerful, carry His message forward, and improve, even in a small way, the lives of everyone I touch. My prayers were, and continue to be, answered in many ways, indeed."

35

RICHARD MONTALTO
Educated to Serve
Deacon, Roman Catholic Church

*Therefore, brothers, be all the more eager to make
your call and election firm, for, in doing so, you will
never stumble. For, in this way, entry into the eternal
kingdom of our Lord and savior Jesus Christ will be
richly provided for you.*

2 Peter 1:10–11

"I always believed that I was 'educated to serve' and was
required to use my God-given time, talent, and treasure for
God's people. One of my favorite sayings was from St.
Teresa of Avila, who essentially said, 'God has no hands
on earth but yours, no eyes on earth but yours, no feet on
earth but yours, and no mouth on earth but yours, so go
forth and do His work.'"

Richard "Monti" Montalto was always meant to "do
His work." He found out early that whatever else he did
with his life, the Lord had a singular expectation of him.

"My most defining Christian moment was my
reception of confirmation when I was told, and believed,
that I was to be a 'soldier for Christ.'"

The real sense of what that was going to mean really
began to come clear while he was being trained to be a
"combatant" during his Army training. Monti carried that

understanding after his discharge and into his collegiate years. While attending Boston College "at the time when it was an Orthodox Catholic university," he came under the direction of the Society of Jesus, also known as the Jesuits.

"It was then that I realized that to be a 'soldier for Christ' I had to be prepared educationally and spiritually in the authentic teachings of Jesus Christ and faithful to the 'chain of command' that He established after His Resurrection."

Monti's "tour of duty" at that point was not in full-time Christian service. The Lord had other plans for Monti, and he was led to them. He entered the insurance field, where he "sold money at a discounted rate." He felt a responsibility to make certain to protect his clients against unforeseen illnesses or accidents. In time he became a broker, feeling a "call" to give himself an even greater opportunity to protect his clients' personal or corporate property and financial assets. "I never looked at a commission schedule and always offered the best product I had at the most competitive price."

Monti's business was taking him back and forth between Maryland and Pennsylvania. He and his wife, Marie, bought a home in Maryland and seemed settled in there. But after a time, they decided that the better location for business reasons was Pennsylvania. So they made the move. It was during this time that Monti was approached and asked to consider the diaconate program that had been reintroduced after Vatican II. There was only one problem—the opportunity was in Maryland.

"I recall telling my wife the information. She said, 'But you're married with a family.' I told her that the permanent diaconate program accepted men who didn't go on to the priesthood. We agreed to pray on it, and one year later I was back in Baltimore."

They moved back, but Monti did not pursue any of the program studies. "I became a workaholic, not only traveling for the company, but training young insurance agents." However, he did volunteer his time, talent, and treasure to his pastor, as he had done with his previous two pastors. But something wasn't right. Monti felt God was trying to say something to him that he was missing. Then one day, he felt a strong message.

"To me the Lord was saying, through Peter, that I had to stop being a 'butterfly.' He was saying that I needed to stop doing what I wanted to do in the church and commit myself permanently to the Lord and let Him lead me, which would eventually mean Paradise."

Then, "due to a strange turn of events," Monti decided to quit his job and go into business for himself as an all-lines insurance broker. At the same time, he made the pledge to pursue his diaconate studies if, and when, he earned enough money to pay for his children's education and cover the family's living expenses. "Two years later, I presented myself to my pastor and requested that he sponsor me to the diaconate program."

The pastor asked Monti to take a year and discern his call. He also assigned a committee to assist with this discernment period. Monti was asked to resign any leadership roles he had on parish committees so that his time would be spent not as a leader but as a servant. To create the time Monti needed to attend classes, study, and continue working, Marie took a night shift job as the RN supervisor in a nursing home.

A committee was set up to evaluate Monti's progress as he prepared for the diaconate. It was a little unusual for a committee to be a part of this process. Monti thought it was curious that his evaluation was being treated differently from those he was familiar with. "A deacon is not a vocation like the priesthood, and scripture is very clear that a deacon is called from the community." Monti understood. He was still working God's plan for his life, and that plan was clear from the beginning. "I was educated to serve."

At the final meeting before his ordination, Monti and

Marie were waiting in church to be called into the group meeting. His advocate came out and said there was a discussion and it would be few more minutes before they would be invited into the meeting. "Marie turned to me and said, 'They aren't going to approve you for ordination.' I said, 'Let's wait and see.'"

Monti was approved. And he received an assignment to serve as deacon at a church in Baltimore, Maryland. At first the relationship with the priest was rocky. But that passed quickly as he and the priest shared laughs and their love for Christ.

"The crowning moment was a time when we were alone in the sacristy and he said, 'I know you will understand what I am going to say, but I never thought you would preach as well as you do.' I could have cried because he was a great preacher. He told me to prepare a homily each week, whether I was assigned to preach or not. I have done that for the twenty-seven years of my diaconate."

St. Teresa of Avila said, "God has no hands on earth but yours, no eyes on earth but yours, no feet on earth but yours, and no mouth on earth but yours, so go forth and do His work."

St. Teresa, meet Monti.

36

JACKIE OSHINSKIE
Fit for God's Use
Co-Owner, Victory Sports & Fitness Club

I can do all things through Christ who strengthens me.

Philippians 4:13

At first, it sounds fairly typical of the kind of mission statement you would find at any fitness club: "Impacting the communities we serve by inspiring and equipping people to live healthier lives..." However, when you read the complete statement, it becomes apparent that the word "Victory" in the name of the facility refers to more than just physical fitness.

"Impacting the communities we serve by inspiring and equipping people to live healthier lives, and serving God by helping His people."

When Jackie Oshinskie and her co-owner husband, Rob, decided to open the club, they thought they were opening something just to fulfill their idea of a fitness facility.

Jackie didn't grow up in an environment that would lead anyone to believe her life would unfold as it has. She was the youngest of three children raised in a middle-class home in the suburbs. So far, typical. At least, during the week.

"My father was what we called a 'weekend alcoholic.'

He and my mother, who both dropped out of high school, fought every weekend, which my siblings and I referred to as the 'weekend fights.' Unfortunately, my dad would get drunk and then beat my mom. Sometimes, as the three of us were hiding, huddled together in one of our bedrooms, we would emerge to what looked like a hurricane had come through our home. Mom stood in the battle, taking the 'hits' to make sure we kids had proper food and clothing, as well as pretty much whatever we wanted. However, emotionally I was insecure and anxious and had very low self-esteem. Of course, spiritually we were as lost as anyone could be."

In the face of all the adverse circumstances in her home life, Jackie was able to attend college and obtain a degree as a nuclear medicine technologist. She worked in the field of nuclear medicine for a total of twelve years at various institutions, including the Hospital of The University of Pennsylvania in Philadelphia, where she specialized in nuclear cardiology. As Jackie reflects on those years, she finds a woman in free-fall.

"I lived for the weekends, when we would party and get drunk. I had the 'token boyfriend.' Although I knew he cared for me, I never felt secure in his love. I had cars, clothes, and money; however, I still felt so unworthy. I lost my father to colorectal cancer when I was twenty-three. Three years later, my brother, whom I was very close to, was killed in a boating accident when he was only twenty-eight. I remember being very mad at God. How could He have taken my brother, who was so well liked and loved life? Somehow I got hold of a booklet that talked about why bad things happen to good people. I believe God was trying to get my attention. Then four years later, while working as a mobile nuclear cardiology tech, I was injured. Eventually, the injuries cost me my job. I was in a five-year relationship that was going nowhere, I had emotional pain and physical pain, and I couldn't seem to get anyone to help me. My world was falling apart around me. I hit rock bottom."

In a search for something to pull her out of despair, twenty-nine-year-old Jackie joined a gym. And it was there that God got her attention in one of His unexpected ways.

"I met Rob at a gym and saw something different in him. Of course, he was handsome and well built. In addition, he had what I describe as a 'shining.' I remember asking him where he got his strength, and to my shock and surprise, he said, 'God.' I never knew anyone who had given God credit for something, and here was a twenty-four-year-old young man who was telling me that God was giving him strength. It blew my mind."

Jackie was drawn to Rob. She made sure Rob knew who she was. And her efforts were rewarded when he became her trainer. But there was a hitch— there was that boyfriend. "Eventually, I broke up with my boyfriend and through 'peer pressure' asked Rob out for a date. Soon, though, I didn't feel worthy of Rob. He seemed so perfect and pure, while I was dirty and unacceptable."

God works in mysterious ways. And Jackie was just about to find out what that means. It began when Jackie invited a friend who was like a big sister to share her apartment. The friendship did not belie the fact that the friend was into drugs and drinking and was involved with a married man. Yet God would work through this very woman to lead Jackie to salvation.

"One day she asked me if I would allow a friend from her work to move in with us. I didn't know it at the time, but he was a backslid Christian. But trusting my friend, I agreed to allow him to move in. We began to have nightly conversations while I was dating Rob, and I told him about my feelings of not being good enough for Rob. One night he told me that Rob was a Christian man and that he was no better than me. He explained to me what that meant since I didn't have a clue! I told him that I wanted what Rob had. He led me in the Sinner's Prayer right there in my living room that night."

Jackie not only got what Rob had; she got Rob. After

four years of dating, they were engaged and subsequently married. The Christian couple settled in State College, Pennsylvania, where he was a strength coach for the Penn State football team. Jackie saw the move as an opportunity to change careers to one that allowed her to have a greater impact in people's lives.

"After much persuasion, I agreed to get certified as a personal trainer. Rob set me up with my first client, the wife of one of his clients. When she showed up, I was a little nervous, of course. But then, before we even started the training, she burst into tears. I ministered to her and found out that she had had a fight with her husband over her son. I convinced her that everything would be okay and that we might as well work out some, since she had already come so far. By the end of the appointment, we were both laughing and having a great time."

When Jackie returned home, she burst through the door and told Rob all about her day and the special encounter with her first client. She asked Rob what he did when a client cried, and Rob said, "I never had a client cry."

"That's when I heard the Holy Spirit tell me that I would attract different clients than Rob. I thought, "I see. I don't have to be just like Rob. He is more like a drill sergeant, and I am more the nurturer."

Now Rob and Jackie were both certified trainers. But more, they were certified trainers receptive to God's voice. That was good because God was ready to use His preparation in their lives to bear witness for Him in a special way. In 2003, Jackie and Rob opened their own fitness center.

"Victory Sports and Fitness. God had been preparing me for this whole time! I used all of the skills I learned in all of my previous jobs to run our business. We thought we were going to just have a place to train people the way we wanted. But God showed us quickly that this is more than a place to work. This is His ministry, and we are His hands and feet."

Little did Jackie Oshinskie know that when she went to the gym that day to tone her body, she was taking with her the Temple of the Holy Spirit. Today, Jackie is fit—for this earthly moment, and for eternity.

37

CAROL A. HILL
The Eternal Third Twine
Cofounder, Friendship Christian Community

*Two are better off than one because together they can
work more effectively. If one of them falls down, the
other can help him up...Two people can resist an
attack that would defeat one person alone. A rope
made of three cords is hard to break.*

Ecclesiastes 4:9

From the beginning, Carol Hill's relationship with Jack was
a "rope made of three cords." Carol is certain of that.

"God gives you the understanding of how important it
is to have Christ as the center of your life. I believe that all
the things I have done were just preparing me to work as a
team with Jack in full-time Christian service."

God's preparation began very early. "I have known the
Lord for many years. At a very young age, I recognized
that God had great plans for my life. When I was twelve
years old, I attended a Baptist Church camp. Even then I
felt God's call to me but really didn't know what to do
about it." God further clarified that for Carol when she
was visiting her Uncle Harold, a Methodist pastor whom
she considers a mentor. "I felt that God was calling me
into youth ministry."

This ministry, as well as other ministries God has led
her into, was part of a life of service Carol had not

anticipated as a wife and mother of two children. Oh, sure, she was active in the Methodist Youth Fellowship (MYF) as a coordinator. She taught Sunday School. In short, she had a full, committed life when its flow was interrupted by divorce and the need to find full-time work. "I worked at the Ocean Bay Diner in Point Pleasant, New Jersey, after my divorce. When the children started school, I worked for the Board of Education as cafeteria manager so I could be home when the children got home."

It was beginning to sound like one of those dead-end stories. But no story is over when someone is entwined with God. "Even when I was alone with my two boys, I knew I was not alone. I felt God was always by my side giving me what I needed to take care of my sons. God was still talking to me, saying, 'I have great plans for you, Carol.'"

Those plans began with an opportunity to direct the youth choir and share direction of the adult choir at the Methodist church she was attending. The codirector was a fellow named Jack Hill. "Before I ever met Jack, he had served his country in World War II. In 1938, Jack had attended Gettysburg College with the thought of going into full-time Christian service. But his education was interrupted with the outbreak of World War II. After the war, Jack went to Lincoln Chiropractic College and got a doctorate in chiropractic. He was also employed by the IRS. In 1962, Jack moved to Lakewood, New Jersey."

And that's where Carol met Jack…and married him. Two cords of three, the Lord cord having already been present when they met. Several years after they were married, Jack and Carol felt that the Lord was speaking to them and leading them to a greater service for Him. "We went on a couples'-weekend spiritual retreat called Marriage Encounter. During the course, we realized that we both wanted to go into full-time Christian ministry."

On their return, they met with their pastor, who encouraged them to speak with the denomination's District Superintendent and the District Committee. "With the sponsorship of the church and the approval of the district, we started down our new path. Jack was immediately assigned as a Lay Pastor of the Forked River United Methodist Church in Forked River, New Jersey. He then enrolled in Wesley Theological Seminary in Washington, DC." The first summer of Jack's studies, Carol was allowed to audit his classes. That costudying venture continued throughout the entire four years they were at Wesley.

"Through this experience at Wesley, I learned a great deal about the profession of pastoring. Jack felt that was enormously helpful to him in his career as a preacher in the United Methodist Church. He was often quoted as saying, 'Carol was enormously helpful to me throughout my career, and I feel that my success was in large measure due to my dear wife, Carol.'"

When Jack completed seminary, he and Carol spent the next six "happy years" building the Forked River Methodist Church from seventy-five people to two hundred and fifty members. They were also instrumental in the purchase of a parsonage for subsequent pastors' families to enjoy.

In June 1985, Carol and Jack retired from the ministry and moved to Zephyrhills, Florida. After just one year of retirement, on July 17, 1986, Pastor Jack Hill found himself leading a new church. "As always, we walked hand in hand in our faith and worked together to build a new church for God's people. Our past had followed us to Florida. The Florida Conference found out what we had done in New Jersey, and there we went again, one more time. I have said many times, 'When God gets a hold of you, He never lets go.' Praise God!"

While Jack was serving the church, Carol worked in sales for a local funeral home. "I was able to go into peoples' homes and help them before someone died. What a great ministry." After a fourth term, the Hills retired again. After just a few months, the District Superintendent called and asked them to pastor a church in another town and save it from closing. Unfortunately, that situation was beyond repair, and the church was closed.

Jack and Carol, comfortable that retirement was now theirs, joined Sebastian UMC. They joined the choir, and she began working at another Methodist church as an after-school program director. While Carol was happy with her job there, she also saw another area of need and decided to address it. "God taps me on the shoulder when He wants me to do something. I try to do what God is asking me to do. Wherever He calls, I will follow." To that end, she and another member founded a new ministry, a Drop-In Center. "We were open every Saturday and on call twenty four-seven for referral services. We also started an Alzheimer's Support Group at Sebastian UMC for both clients and caregivers."

Carol's life remained active wherever God placed her and her beloved Jack. Then, on August 4, 2008, the Lord called Jack home, leaving Carol and her sons without a husband and father, but not without faith. "Even after I lost Jack, I knew I was not alone. I felt God was always by my side. God was still talking to me, saying, 'I have great plans for you, Carol.'" And He did.

Carol and a group of friends have been instrumental in founding Friendship Christian Community and serving in a number of capacities to vitalize its programs. Her generosity with her time and talent spreads beyond her church activities. In collaboration with several physicians, Carol started Friendship Medical and Family Counseling Services, a nonprofit, community-based organization with programs designed to promote the development of emotionally, physically, and spiritually healthy individuals throughout the Treasure Coast of Florida.

When Jack was called home to his great reward, the second cord was broken. Through God's strength and Carol's faith, the rope remained firm. Understanding the need for others who have suffered the loss of a spouse, she has been instrumental in helping them heal, creating a support group called The Sunshine Group. "I started The Sunshine Group after my husband died as a way to help other men and women to grow in their faith. I also wanted to give each person the opportunity to share where they were in their grief and to move forward to Christ being the center of their lives by trusting that the Lord still has a purpose for them. We have used the book *The Purpose Driven Life* by Rick Warren to help them discover what God put them on this planet to do. There's nothing quite like it. I am excited because I know all of the great things that are going to happen to them. They happened to me, and I have never been the same since I discovered the purpose for my life. God has been so good to me. I feel He is still training me for what is to come. I have been able to help many people because of what I have been through in my life. Is there any other way to live?"

Carol remained hopeful that the Lord would someday provide a new "second cord" in her life. In the summer of 2015, this prayer was answered, when God again sent her that third cord to work in partnership with her in Christian ministry.

"His name is Doug, and while his background is different to my own experiences, having a Catholic background, he is so willing to serve the Lord and to help people. He not only 'talks the talk; he walks the walk,' and he is willing to walk by my side in the ministry. Praise be to God."

Doug shares Carol's affinity for answering God's call. He participates in community and church-affiliated services such as Daily Bread, Faith Unity Evangelism Leadership (FUEL), and the men's retreat at his church, Ascension Catholic Church.

Carol is once again part of the rope that is complete just as God ordained. "A rope made of three cords." A rope that is hard to break.

38

PETER ACKERMAN
Good-Bye, H'wood; Hello, God
Episcopal Priest

I can do all things through Christ who strengthens me.

Philippians 4:13

"I serve a God of whom there is much mystery, so everything is unusual, while at the same time nothing is!"

Peter Ackerman is a testament to the truth of his statement, right from the beginning of his life.

"I feel that I have always been in the Lord. No joke, I was born a few hours after my pregnant and married mother was baptized as an adult at an Episcopal Church. After the service, her water broke, and she went to the hospital, where I was born on Easter Sunday."

It was appropriate that Peter's life should begin in such a dramatic way. He grew up in a "show-biz" family. His father was the executive producer of a popular television series. His mother, who was an actress, was well known at the time. Although he grew up with show-business parents, he calls himself fortunate that they raised their children "as a 'regular family,' not entitled youth of privilege, which we weren't anyway, but children of parents who worked."

As Peter began sorting out career options, he decided to follow in his mother's footsteps and become an actor.

He acted in a couple of episodes of the last television series on which his father was executive producer. "But I spent most of that time as a waiter. The benefit of that time period is that I met my wife, Marie."

During the years Peter spent "hanging around" with his father, he had an opportunity to see the other side of the camera where so much of the work happens to create the TV show. Eventually, he was drawn to that side of the camera, too. After his father died in 1991, he spent most of his work time in production for TV commercials, music videos, and later on television shows.

"I was never involved in the creative stuff but always was one of the guys working behind the scenes."

It was this work, with its long and irregular hours, that began to have an impact on Peter's church life and faith. Although he had been confirmed and even married in the same church he was baptized in, things began to change. "My light was drifting away." However, his return to faith was as dramatic as his exit had been undramatic.

"After being held up at gunpoint, while holding my infant son, I reassessed my life as I was living it at the time, and with the direction of the Holy Spirit found my way one Sunday to the Episcopal Church near the neighborhood where I was living at the time. That is where I reengaged my faith journey in a palpable way."

Peter, now a husband and father, returned to the journey he had wandered away from earlier. It began by simply volunteering to usher at his church. That led to accepting greater roles in the church's programs. Even while Peter was still working in the television industry, the parish asked him to become its paid Youth Leader and then its Parish Administrator. It was the parishioners in this church who, witnessing God at work through Peter, first pointed out that God was calling him to become an Episcopal priest.

"I have always learned to listen to how God speaks through others. That, coupled with the fact that I loved working in a parish setting even more than on a hit TV show, caused me to listen and humbly take the steps to discern if what I was hearing was truly a calling."

Peter heeded the call to ordained ministry because of things happening in his life that confirmed his decision. When he hit figurative walls, they were removed. For instance, he realized that for him to eventually go to seminary, he had to finish his undergraduate degree, which he had left at the two-year mark. So Peter went back to the local community college he had attended to pick up where he left off, only to learn that his credits were no longer valid. He would have to take the equivalent of three and a half years' worth of courses. And he would have to do it part time while he was working, adding even more years to complete a degree.

"It was enough to make me give up. When I was telling this to my priest in casual conversation, a woman who had just been hired at the church office overheard this and told us about her friend who worked at the very college I was trying to get into. His sole job was to 'grandfather' people in who once had met college requirements. On her suggestion, I made a call to her friend, and in two weeks' time, I was enrolled as a junior at the university. The Holy Spirit was lifting all obstacles, so I kept walking forward, heeding the call."

Today, Peter the actor is Peter the priest, serving as the solo priest at a congregation and as a rector in a dual role, both administrative and pastoral. Besides the usual preaching, teaching, and leading a variety of services, he chairs the vestry and oversees parish communications as well as the day-to-day operations of the church and the preschool associated with it. And Peter has found that the "actor" years still play a role in his ministry.

"Ironically, or maybe not, when I began junior college in the early 1980s, they didn't have 'camera acting' courses, so I had to be stage-trained. So I learned early how to project my voice and present my public persona. I am one of the few people I know who actually likes speaking in front of others. In addition, a course such as improvisation helps me when I work with dementia patients, as a way of being present with them wherever they are in their realities."

Peter Ackerman might have been an actor, a director, or a producer. But God had other plans.

"Why me as a priest? I do not know, but it fits with what God's higher purpose is, so I do not question it."

39

BILL MCCARTHY
Erinn's Gift
Executive Director of Catholic Charities,
Baltimore, Maryland

Then the King will say to those on his right hand,
"Come, you blessed of my Father, inherit the kingdom
prepared for you from the foundation of the world: for I
was hungry and you gave me food; I was thirsty and
you gave me drink; I was a stranger and you took me
in; I was naked and you clothed me; I was sick and
you visited me; I was in prison and you came to me."
Then the righteous will answer him, saying, "Lord,
when did we see you hungry and feed you, or thirsty
and give you drink? When did we see you a stranger
and take you in, or naked and clothed you? Or when
did we see you sick, or in prison, and come to you?"
And the King will answer and say to them,
"Assuredly, I say to you, inasmuch as you did it to one
of the least of these my brethren, you did it to me."
Mathew 25:34–40

"Erinn's gift to all of us is that life is a gift. Live each day
with a purpose. Focus on things that you can do and leave
to God and others those things you cannot."

It was with those words Bill McCarthy closed his
eulogy for his daughter, fourteen-year-old Erinn
McCarthy. Until Erinn was diagnosed with cancer, life had

unfolded for Bill McCarthy the way he wished it to.

Bill's family moved to Baltimore, Maryland, when he was very young. He still lives in Baltimore. He and his wife of twenty-five years, Maria, have made a conscious choice to stay right where they are. It was one of two requirements Bill demanded of his career decisions.

"In spite of many amazing opportunities to do so, I never wanted to leave Baltimore, the community where Maria and I had spent our lives, the place where we loved, had roots, and both of our families lived. All of our friends were here, and so were the institutions that formed us and were so important to us."

The second requirement was equally important because of the kind of man Bill is.

"I had to be actively engaged in our community, in service to both others and to organizations. I was actively involved in my church, schools, nonprofits, and business organizations."

Bill came by this strong sense of benevolence naturally.

"My parents were amazing at modeling, in teaching my sisters and me the importance of service and being active in your community, whether it's church, school, neighborhood, or the broader community. I have been active in service and the community since I was very young. I learned very early how personally enriching service and community engagement are."

Bill attended Catholic schools from elementary school through college, including postgraduate and law schools. "Everything I have done reflects the Jesuit formation of 'men for others' I received at Loyola High School." Bill eventually graduated from Seton Hall with a law degree and finished his master's degree in taxation. After law school, he joined a local law firm, where he focused on planning and business transactions. Maria settled into her job as a pharmacist at St. Joseph's Medical Center. And a cascade of more good events rushed into Bill's life.

"Our daughter, Erinn, was born first. When our son,

Ryan, was born three years later, I had the opportunity to leave private practice and go into banking. I ultimately led the Trust Company and Wealth Management Division of First National Bank."

His rise through the ranks was not fate. "I always loved what I did and where I did it. When my love and passion for what I was doing waned, I would change what I did. I never let what I did define who I was as a person."

When First National merged with M&T Bank, Bill moved to SunTrust Bank, where, in time, he became President of the Maryland Division. While he was making this rise through the ranks of banking, Bill never allowed it to temper his charitable work.

"I was energized and enriched by giving of myself and always sought to do more. I wanted to live each day with greater purpose."

By his own admission, he was blessed "with an amazing family and better friends than I deserve."

Bill McCarthy's life was, by all standards, what every man desires his to be: beloved husband and father, good friend and neighbor, successful businessman, philanthropic with his time and talent, and happy with his lot in life. Most important, he was strong in his love of the Lord. "I have always been a man of great faith."

Now that faith was to be tested...distressingly so. The orthopedist the McCarthys had been seeing about a pain in Erinn's leg suspected that she might have cancer in that leg. When they arrived for a scheduled visit, he had already set up another appointment with an oncologist at the Johns Hopkins Hospital.

"In December 2003, we received news that no parent should have to hear and all parents fear. Our daughter, Erinn, age eleven at the time, was diagnosed with osteosarcoma, a rare form of bone cancer. She had been having some difficulty in the fall with vision and leg pain, but we did not imagine this."

On Christmas Eve, they were at the hospital for tests

and to meet with the treatment team to discuss the chemotherapy treatment Erinn would be taking. Bill and Maria knew that what was to follow was going to be tough.

"Even so, we had a plan. We had hope and felt blessed to be in a community with the medical resources like Johns Hopkins."

Over the next ten months, Erinn had thirty-five weeks of treatment during twenty stays at the hospital. Maria would stay with Erinn, even sleeping in her room every time Erinn was admitted. "Maria is also my hero." Eventually, employing all the physical and mental strength she could muster, and approaching life with determination and a positive attitude, Erinn returned to school.

"We celebrated the end of treatment and return to school with what Erinn called a 'life is great; let's celebrate' party at the end of October."

The family leaned on Erinn's positive attitude and their faith to sustain them, even as the disease got worse. On March 16, 2007, Erinn began her new life in heaven. Over the next two years, Bill and Maria established and led a campaign that raised $12.5 million to construct the new Erinn McCarthy Humanities Hall at Maryvale, the school she had attended and that gave Erinn exceptional support.

"It was through Erinn's example of faith and living each day with courage, grace, and purpose that made me strive to do more, to live each day with greater purpose, to help our neighbors in need, and to make our community better."

The desire to make lives better for those in need was more than a personal goal; it was God refreshing His call to service. Only now, it was to be accomplished through a specific role. Instead of participating as a charity-organization volunteer, Bill was to lead one.

"I took over as executive director of Catholic Charities of Baltimore approximately two years after Erinn's passing. With twenty three hundred colleagues and nearly twenty thousand volunteers, Catholic Charities annually assists hundreds of thousands of our neighbors in need. We serve people living in poverty, children and families in crisis, individuals with intellectual disabilities, seniors, and our new neighbors, the immigrant community."

Bill approached the new position incorporating a business framework into the charitable structure that already existed. As a businessman with a strong faith based in the Gospel, he was comfortable in this role, which he was certain was God's calling.

"I know I was called to make a difference. This job is personally enriching. More important, it is very gratifying to know I am working to make a difference in lives every day. We are living the Gospel and bringing Christ to people."

Bill has made many modifications to the organization, including changing the mission statement from what the organization is to what it does. Today the statement is "Inspired by the Gospel mandates to love, serve, and teach, Catholic Charities provides care and services to improve the lives of Marylanders in need."

The organizational mission statement is also an apt description of Bill McCarthy's personal mission he has lived by since he was old enough to understand "service." It is also his outward expression of Erinn's gift: "Live each day with a purpose."

ABOUT THE AUTHOR

Water Walkers is Vince Clews's first book. He began his career as a scriptwriter, and eventually producer, for public television. He created and produced the popular PBS series *Consumer Survival Kit*. Vince spent the next several decades writing and producing video scripts for the clients of his production company, Vince Clews & Associates. His work has taken him around the world, including visits to many remote areas, where he has seen both a need for the message of salvation and, at the same time, the blessings of receiving it.

In 2013, Vince required, and was blessed by the results of, a heart transplant. He continues in good health under the special care of the University of Maryland Medical Center's cardiac care team, especially the unit headed by Dr. Erika Feller.

Vince is an Orthodox Anglican, the central word being Orthodox.

If you are aware of a story that fits the profile of those in *Water Walkers*, please contact the author at vinceclews@comcast.net. Vince is currently starting work on *More Water Walkers*.

Ron Esposito

Made in the USA
Middletown, DE
27 April 2016